CONFESSIONS
OF A RECOVERING RACIST

WHAT WHITE PEOPLE MUST DO TO OVERCOME RACISM IN AMERICA

LOU SNEAD

Printed in the United States of America
ISBN: 978-1-956019-06-3 (paperback)
ISBN: 978-1-956019-07-0 (ebook)

Canoe Tree
Press

4697 Main Street
Manchester Center, VT 05255

Canoe Tree Press is a division of DartFrog Books.

"White people in this country have to find out in their hearts why it was necessary for them to invent the 'nigger.'"

—James Baldwin

"It is an aspect of their sense of superiority that the white people of America believe they have so little to learn."

—Martin Luther King, Jr.

CONTENTS

PREFACE

This book is written for those like me who racially identify themselves as being White and who realize that racism in America remains a nagging problem we have never adequately addressed. My hope is to add to the conversations going on today about what Whites can or must do to eradicate the vestiges of racial biases that continue to undermine our nation's ideals of liberty, equality, and justice for all.

Drawing on my own struggle to free myself from my childhood racial indoctrination and working for decades to address racial inequities and injustices, I believe that those of us who are White need to accept the responsibility for overcoming the legacy of racism that still plagues America. As someone who has undergone a serious transformation in my racial awareness, I recognize this is not an easy proposition for a lot of Whites to accept. Our emotional resistance to addressing racial issues has been described in a variety of ways: White fragility, White rage, and White denial, just to name a few. Some of this discomfort is easy to understand. Many of us remember the indignities, the abuses, the injustices, and the violence that White people inflicted on people with darker skin colors during the civil rights era of the 1950s and 1960s. These memories have a way of stirring up feelings of shame, guilt, and remorse for many of us who are White. Others of us like to believe that the worse forms of racism have been eliminated today, so they resist the suggestion that we may still harbor or perpetuate some degree of a White racial bias.

Over the past few years, however, our awareness of the persistence of White racial biases has been starkly brought to our attention via first-hand news reports, cell phone videos, and dashboard cameras. We have been forced to see troubling examples of Whites shooting unarmed Black men and White people acting in racially discriminatory ways toward People of Color. The amount of racially motivated violence that took place between the tragic murders of African Americans attending a church Bible study in Charleston in 2015 and the shooting of Latinos in a Walmart in El Paso in 2019 should have been enough to dispel any notion that we have escaped the clutches of racism in this country. More recently, the 2020 murders of Breonna Taylor, Ahmaud Arbery, and George Floyd have suddenly galvanized America's awareness that racial issues continue to haunt our nation. While these contemporary examples of racial violence and discrimination are nothing new in this country, social media has simply made us more aware of the brutality, callousness, and inhumanity of racist actions against People of Color. The resurgence of White nationalism and White supremacy groups since the election of President Trump in 2016 only underscores this awareness that problematic racial issues still exist in America. The White Ilusion that we are living in a post-racial America has been shattered even more recently by the January 6, 2021 insurrection of White supremacists carrying Confederate flags in our nation's Capital and by the number of Asian Americans who have been targeted by racial violence. I believe we are now at an important inflection point where those of us who have White skin have to ask ourselves what we can do to purge ourselves and our nation of the legacy of forty or more generations of racism in America.

The premise of this book rests on two convictions: (1) In order to completely eliminate racism in this country, those of us who are White must be willing to examine how our conscious and unconscious racial biases, along with our White privileges, continue to perpetuate racial disparities and injustices that negatively affect non-Whites, and (2) White people must work at ridding ourselves, both individually and collectively, of the ideology of white superiority that has been so pervasive in our cultural history and in many of our public policies and institutions. I believe that until we can free ourselves from our inherited White racial biases and privileges, we will never embody "the Beloved Community" that Dr. Martin Luther King, Jr. imagined where people are judged by the content of their character rather than the color of their skin.

These convictions are rooted in both my personal experience with racism and my commitment to becoming an anti-racist. What I have learned about addressing racial biases has been informed by my forty years of experience serving as the pastor of White, affluent congregations in several major cities. I have also been inspired by the growing numbers of those who recognize that the anti-racism challenge we face today rests with those of us who have inherited cultural biases and social practices that benefit Whites while negatively impacting People of Color. So, the racial bias recovery process I am advocating in this book will require a serious measure of introspection on the part of every White person. In the same way the Alcoholics Anonymous program approaches addiction recovery, I contend that the first step in overcoming our White racial biases is the acknowledgment that *we* have a problem. Those of us who are White-skinned people in America have to carefully examine how we may have acquired in varying degrees "the color line problem"—the relation of darker to lighter skin colors—that W. E. B. DuBois described over a hundred years ago.

Some readers will likely think I am projecting too much of my personal experiences with racism onto all White people. This may be true to some extent. I know many White people have been spared from the kind of heavy racist indoctrination I received in my childhood—an indoctrination that I have had to work diligently to overcome. However, my active involvement with community racial reconciliation efforts over the past several decades has led me to believe that White racial biases are still very much alive among many of us, often in latent and naïve ways. Many of us simply do not recognize or acknowledge how our White racial biases may inhabit us in subtle and unconscious ways.

To get at these more hidden aspects of racism, I invite the reader to explore the two challenges raised years ago by James Baldwin and Dr. Martin Luther King about the roots of White racial biases that we must address and eradicate. In this regard, overcoming our racial biases about People of Color is not limited just to African Americans. Latinos, Asians, Native Americans, and other ethnic groups have also experienced racial discrimination and inequities because they were not considered to be "White." Let me add this quick word of encouragement. To engage in this kind of racial awareness process, it will be necessary for Whites to first check our racial defensiveness at the door before we attempt to address these challenges.

In writing this book, I am indebted to a wide range of voices, some White and many by People of Color, who have expanded my own racial self-awareness. Many good books have been written in the past few years to address the dynamics and complexity of racism in America. Race awareness training programs have also added to this White "awakening." Drawing on a cadre of academic research and reflective engagement with racism, I have learned a great deal about my own racial biases that I long tried to ignore.

I am especially grateful for those who have studied and written extensively about the dynamics of white superiority and white privilege upon whom I have drawn much of this book. In recent years there has also been growing recognition within public institutions, private corporations, and faith communities of the value of cultural competency and implicit bias training. Many of us have benefitted from conversations with People of Color who are teaching us how to become anti-racists. Most Whites, however, have not been exposed to either the academic studies, the racial awareness training, or the conversations that address how White racial biases and racist policies impact People of Color. So, in writing this book, I have attempted to incorporate some of these understandings about the social structures of racial biases and the history of racist ideas into the recovery orientation I am promoting for Whites like me. In the last chapters, I offer some pragmatic suggestions and resources that are available to help Whites address and overcome our racial biases, both in terms of our individual attitudes and behavior as well as institutional racist practices and policies. That said, the resources I have found helpful to me and that I recommend to others are not an all-inclusive list, nor are these necessarily the best available resources. So, I encourage you to discover resources that may be more helpful to you. In terms of references cited in this work, I trust I have made the contributions of all my sources of inspiration and understanding obvious to the reader in the chapters and in the Notes of this book.

Since language is always important, allow me to make two statements about the words I use in this book. First, I want to apologize in advance to my readers for the inclusion of White racist epithets and demeaning characterizations of People of Color in my personal confession. I was reluctant to use this offensive, racist language in recounting my racist indoctrination but decided to do so to demonstrate how thoroughly immersed I was in overt White racism in my early years. I hope the use of this language will not be an obstacle for my readers in appreciating the honest racial bias recovery process I am promoting in this book. Secondly, the reader will notice that I have capitalized the terms often used to convey racial identities based on old notions about skin color markers: White, Black, Latino, Asian, etc. I am very aware that these racial identification terms no longer fit for those who are mixed-race or for those like myself who resist being asked to identify ourselves in these old racial terms. Nevertheless, these racial identities continue to shape our conversations today about race. So, I will use the term "White" to refer to those of us who have European ancestry and are often classified as "Caucasians" and will use the general term "People of Color" or "BIPOC" to refer to those who are otherwise identified as "African American/Black," "Latinos/Latinx," "Indigenous/Native American," and "Asian."

INTRODUCTION

"Among the moral imperatives of our time, we are challenged to work all over the world with unshakable determination to wipe out the last vestiges of racism."

—Martin Luther King, Jr.

My name is Lou, and I am a recovering racist. This admission is to let the reader know that I have been engaged in a life-long struggle to free myself from the ideology of white superiority that I learned as a child growing up in the South. By identifying myself this way, I am also recognizing I have made enormous strides in overcoming the deeply embedded white racial biases that have characterized racism in America for generations. This book has emerged out of my efforts to confront these White racial biases, both within myself and in the White communities in which I have lived. Like anyone who is trying to recover from a disease or a moral failure, the healing process is rarely easy. My own experiences with White racial biases and White privilege have made me aware of the many challenges that most White people in America face when we honestly look at how our racial biases and privileges benefit us while diminishing People of Color. In the past year alone, a growing number of Whites have come to realize that racial inequities still exist in this country. However, many of us are far less aware of how our inherited and collective racial biases contribute to this reality.

This book is an invitation to White people to explore how old ideas about racial identity continue to create racial injustices and inequities to this day and how we can overcome the twin evils of White superiority and White privilege. I must warn you at the outset, what you will discover in this racism recovery process may make you uncomfortable, anxious, and angry. In fact, this book will likely not be helpful to those of us who minimize the importance of race in America today and who conveniently live in White communities with little or no personal contact with People of Color. So, the Whites who read the perspective I am offering will need to bring along some courage, intellectual honesty, and vulnerability about racial issues with you.

I begin with the assumption that those of us who know anything about our nation's history can acknowledge our troubled past with White racism. The genocide of Native Americans by White European settlers, the enslavement of Africans for cheap labor on agricultural plantations, the violence and oppression directed at Negroes and Mexican Americans during the Jim Crow era, and the White resistance to ending racial segregation during the civil rights era all stand together as ugly testimonies to America's racist history. We can add to this sordid history the racial biases and injustices toward Chinese immigrants in the nineteenth century and toward Japanese citizens during World War II, along with discriminatory attitudes toward a host of other ethnic groups to this day. Given the racial roots of this unpleasant history, it doesn't take much intellectual honestly to understand why I claim that racism is essentially a White ethnicity problem.

As much as we may try to overlook the past, we cannot sanitize our nation's ugly history of White racial discrimination and racial injustices nor claim this history has no real connection to racial inequities and injustices today. Many of us who are White often want to distance ourselves from this racist history and disassociate ourselves from its legacy. But there is no escaping the clutches that White racial biases have had in shaping our nation to this day. Perhaps for this reason alone, addressing the subject of racism today is for many White people like pulling a scab off an old wound that has not healed. Some of us prefer to believe that the tragic impact of this racist history will need to heal on its own over time. Most Whites today recoil from any suggestion that we are somehow implicated in this socially constructed disease that our White culture has perpetuated for generations. So, the perspective offered here will be hard for many Whites to accept, much less to embrace. While I will argue that none of us may be personally responsible for creating racist ideas and practices, all of us who are White are nevertheless the cultural inheritors of White racial biases and privileges that continue to reveal themselves in individuals, our communities, and our institutions.

Laying our nation's longstanding problems with racism at the feet of White people often evokes all sorts of negative reactions—anger, guilt, resentment, and massive disagreement. My intention in this book is not to condemn all White people as racists. Rather, my goal is to help those of us who are White to discover whatever embedded, latent, or unconscious racial biases we may have acquired in order to dismantle the racism in America that still persists. Admittedly, this exploration requires an openness to rethinking some of the ideas we may have about the nature of racism and how White superiority has and continues to function socially and culturally and within our nation's institutions. The immediate difficulty that many Whites have today with this kind of examination is our resistance to the idea that we might still harbor as individuals some form of a White racial bias. Even more challenging is the suggestion that most of us may be complicit in ignoring racist public policies and injustices that continue to occur. Simply acknowledging the pervasive and subtle racial biases that frequently show up among Whites today is, in itself, exceedingly difficult for some of us.

As most People of Color know, White people often become very defensive whenever someone suggests that Whites own the problem of racism. Some of this defensiveness is understandable. We typically reserve the label "racist" for those White people who make up the KKK, White supremacist groups, or who sound like bigoted White individuals who detest People of Color. Since the 1970s, most of us who are White have been quick to distance ourselves from those who spew racist vitriol and disrespect toward People of Color. On the whole, the White community in America today believes "racism" is a misguided social attitude from the past about the inferiority of non-White people. And many White people, like me, have worked at freeing ourselves from the stains of overt White racism that we may have inherited from past generations. We can also be thankful that younger generations of Whites today have been spared from the harsher brands of racism that existed just fifty to sixty years ago when there were "White" and "Colored" signs on restrooms and water fountains and racially segregated schools. Nevertheless, conversations I have had in recent years with both White people and People of Color about racial issues indicate that very few of us have been completely inoculated against the germs of White racial biases as a socially acquired disease carried by generations of White Americans. As with the stigma of having any "social disease," most White people today want to preserve our personal virtues as non-racists rather than admit we may still possess some racist contamination in us.

Before you think I am painting White racism in America with too broad of a brush, let me offer this caveat. There is no doubt that

White people, on the whole, have made significant progress since the civil rights era in moving beyond the overt forms of White racism that were commonplace a generation or two ago. This has certainly been true for me, as my confessional examples of overcoming my White racial biases will demonstrate. And, yes, our nation has made significant progress in overcoming the gross racial inequalities, injustices, and inequities that existed in the past. Thanks to the enlightened public policies adopted over the past sixty years, many of the most egregious barriers and injustices of racial segregation and discrimination have been removed. Having an African American president serve our nation for two terms, along with now having an African American female vice president, represent important milestones in this endeavor. While racial progress has definitely been made, it has been exceedingly slow, and racial equality by most measures has not been achieved. The tragic murders of unarmed Black men caught on cell phones that led to the Black Lives Matter movement have "woke" many Whites today to the problems that grow out of our racial biases. Moreover, the photo of a White man carrying a Confederate flag in the rotunda of the Capitol during the insurrection on January 6, 2021, is a sobering reminder we still have a lot of work to do to purge our nation of the ideology of White supremacy. I contend that future progress toward racial equity and justice will require more of us who are White to deal with the difficult challenges involved in overcoming embedded racial biases and undoing the remnants of structural racism. Until we address the roots of White racism, our conscious and unconscious notions about White superiority, and the continuing effects of White privilege, we may never reach the moral ideals and equality goals we all claim we want to achieve in America.

I know from my own experience that addressing the issue of race is difficult for most of us who are White. Just talking about racism makes many of us very uncomfortable and anxious. Most of us resist any suggestion that we may condone racism in any form as individuals or as a society. In our rush to distance ourselves from the subject, many of us have become almost blind, or at least naive, about how White racial biases continue to hold a grip on us. We prefer to believe that we are living today in a more equitable society where People of Color now have the same opportunities that White people do. And in some identifiable ways, this is true. At the same time, it is difficult to ignore the experiences that People of Color continue to report about how White racial biases still show up in their lives and in our communities. In national surveys and local conversations, those who should be the authorities on the prevalence of White racism—People of Color—continue to say, almost unequivocally, that racism is still alive and well in America. The deaths of Breonna Taylor, Ahmaud Arbery, and George Floyd just in the past year should have dispelled any belief that our country has moved beyond racial injustices. Reports about racial biases in law enforcement and the mistreatment of People of Color in coffee shops and public parks, along with stories about fearful reactions to the presence of Black people in White neighborhoods, all indicate the presence of lingering racial biases that show up regularly to this day. These racial "incidences" often upend our moral sensibilities and challenge our perceptions that America has cleansed itself of the perniciousness of White racial biases and racial inequities. When we listen to the experiences of Black and Brown-skinned people, we discover that racial equality and the end of widespread racial prejudices is a false narrative that only White people prefer to embrace. People of Color know full well that White bigotry and racial discrimination can raise their ugly heads at almost any time and any place in America today, often with deadly consequences.

Another indication of our resistance to addressing racial issues becomes apparent whenever conversations arise about our nation's history with racism. These conversations make many White people not only uncomfortable but also defensive. Yes, we might acknowledge that racism has been America's Achilles heel in terms of our ability to embody the principles of freedom, equality, and justice that we like to claim this nation was founded upon. We may even understand why racism has been called America's "original sin," from which we are still struggling to overcome.

Many of us are painfully aware of the tragic history of slavery and the brutality that People of Color have experienced at the hands of White people in this country for generations. And many Whites have developed a great deal of sympathy toward the suffering, the gross injustices, and the family disintegration that White racism has created for People of Color in our country for hundreds of years. Yet, this history of racism, like the subject of racism itself, stirs up a host of negative emotional reactions from those of us who are White. Despite two presidents, one White and one Black, imploring us over the past twenty-five years to have a national conversation about racial issues, very few of us seem interested in or willing to talk about the manifestations of White racial biases, even though racially charged issues keep occurring all around this country almost daily.

Meanwhile, surveys about racial issues in America continue to indicate that there are significant differences between Whites and Blacks in terms of race relations, racial equality, and racial discrimination in America today. The 2018 Pew Research Study on race revealed that 71 percent of Blacks believe race relations in the U.S. are bad while only 56 percent of Whites agree with them. Even more troubling is the perception among a smaller percentage of Whites (37 percent) that our country has not done enough for equal rights among the races, while a large majority of Blacks (78 percent) believe not enough has been done. When asked about their experience with racial discrimination, 76 percent of Blacks and Asians alike say they have had such experiences, and 58 percent of Latinos say so as well. However, 67 percent of Whites say they never see racial discrimination against People of Color. These statistics alone suggest that White perceptions about racism do not reflect the realities for People of Color in this country.

Ironically, many of us like to claim we are racially enlightened and have now become "colorblind" regarding race. This illusion was bolstered in the 2008 election and then the re-election of Barack Obama as the first African American president of the United States of America. It became easy for White America to assume that this election somehow signaled the end of racism in this country. Our White optimism and hopefulness about the end of racism, however, was shattered by the frequency and circumstances of the killings of People of Color around the country during President Obama's terms in office. Many of us have been shocked and saddened by what appears to be unwarranted assaults and shootings of dark-skinned citizens.

The frequency of questionable, if not unjustified, shootings of young Black men by police officers confirmed for many White people the truth about the perceptions among African Americans that racism continues to play a huge role in how law enforcement is carried out in this country. Over the past year, the ongoing examples of White violence and the racist killings of People of Color have galvanized a greater awareness of racial injustices among a growing number of White people today. The re-emerging public demonstrations by White supremacist and White Nationalist groups remind us that ardent racists still exist among us. The evil of racism has now reappeared in ways that upend our hopefulness about transcending old racist ideas and practices. Protests by Blacks and Whites against racist police practices have filled the streets of many of our cities and around the world.

Conflicts over continuing to give Confederate monuments public places of honor have revealed a renewed awareness about the desire of some Whites to protect old racial symbols. Many of us now believe that Donald Trump's presidency represented an appeal to latent White biases that had simply gone underground for a while. All of these racial issues have forced some of us to re-examine the roots of White racism with the desire to remove the continued stranglehold that racism has had on our nation. This book is the result of that kind of re-examination of White racism, at both a personal level and among White Americans in general.

In seeking to become an anti-racist, the first question that I had to ask myself is: **What racial biases have I acquired and might still possess unconsciously that I need to confront?** From my own experience, I believe this question of personal self-examination is the doorway to eradicating the White racial biases and the racial disparities that still exist in our country today. The trajectory I will follow in this book begins with defining "racism" and illustrating from my own personal history how White racial biases are most often inherited and appropriated without question. In one sense, this is a White person's recognition and acknowledgment of how racial biases often shape our lives in ways that we do not consciously realize or even intend to adopt. My confession is also an acknowledgment that my racial prejudices continue to show up in me in ways that I am sometimes unaware of or don't like to admit. I know there are other White people who recognize we have "inherited" racist views and attitudes simply through cultural assimilation rather than by any intention of our own. As my personal history will reveal, escaping the clutches of White racial biases passed on to us in social attitudes from the past about People of Color, along with understanding the benefits that White skin brings to us, constitute the primary challenge that many Whites face today.

The racial bias recovery process outlined in this book asks us to recognize the pervasiveness of racial biases that still exist in America today and to move beyond the denial and defensiveness many of us exhibit when the subject of racism comes up. Part of this effort requires us to get beyond the binary definitions of racism that create our defensiveness and resistance.

Drawing upon the work of many others who have addressed White racism and White racial biases, I will try to unpack the complexities that often accompany implicit and embedded racial biases. The core of this book will consist of an examination of the roots of the "Whiteness" standard that I believe we must address in order to dismantle whatever racial biases we can identify. Since I believe that White people have to accept the responsibility for eradicating our racial biases and behavior, I provide in the last chapters some practical ways for White people to explore both our individual racial awareness as well as the systemic forms of White racial biases that are still entrenched in our nation. Coming to terms with our own racial biases, as unconscious or innocent as these may be, is the first step in this process of undoing racism.

So, my confessional approach to undoing our racial biases underscores the importance of coming to terms with our personal and collective history regarding White racism in its varying forms as a means to recognizing its roots in White superiority and privilege. Let's recognize up front that some of the resistance among White people today to engage in conversations about race grows out of the fact that we didn't choose the color of our skin, and we should not be condemned for simply being White in America. Racial biases are, nonetheless, complicated for many of us simply because the ubiquity of our skin color prevents us from seeing how race impacts our lives. So, I will address how our Whiteness often leads us to assume our biases are racially neutral rather than racially privileged.

As I have said, the goal of this book is to help White people work at freeing themselves from the ideology of White superiority, from our White privilege, and from systemic racism. In the last chapters and appendix, I will offer some practical steps that any White person can take to identify and unpack whatever latent and unconscious racial biases that may reside within ourselves. At the end of the book, you will find some resources that I found in my experience that White communities can use to address racial inequities and injustices that arise in our nation's structures and institutions with the aim of becoming anti-racists.

Let me state here the core belief on which this book rests. It is my conviction that those of us who are White must ultimately come to terms with the origins, intentions, and impacts of the ideology of White superiority and White privilege that has been deeply ingrained in our culture. As I hope to make clear, when I use the term "racism," I am referring to more than our tendency to make negative judgments about people simply on the basis of skin color and a few other physical attributes. **I define *racism* as the systematic, institutionalized devaluation and mistreatment of one group of people by another group based primarily on biases about racial identities and ancestral backgrounds. Implied in this definition is the recognition that racial discrimination becomes racial oppression when one racial group has the social, political, and economic power to impose their attitudes and biases on others.** White people, of course, do not have the exclusive right to holding racial biases. But White people in this country have historically had the power to create a perceptual prejudicial notion about White superiority and to under-gird this racial prejudice with personal and institutional power to use against

People of Color. Consequently, White racism has long been part of the social DNA of America, whether we like to acknowledge it or not. I contend that most of us who have been shaped in America's White culture have inherited to some degree aspects of the old racial bias that implies a White racial identity is somehow superior to other racial identities. I only ask the reader to explore with me how these culturally acquired racial biases may show up in each of us individually and in the economic, political, and social institutions under which we live. By becoming more aware of our White racial biases, we are better prepared to become the anti-racists we need to be.

In attempting to address the uncomfortable subject of White racism, I have drawn upon the research and insights of many others who have examined in-depth the dynamics of White superiority that lies at the heart of our racial conditioning. As the sociologist Joe Feagin has pointed out, White people who dare to address racism in the U.S. must acknowledge two historically uncontested realities: First, the racial oppression of People of Color has been institutionalized and rationalized in the fabric of White America for twenty generations or more. Second, the racial inequalities that exist today, as seen in the gaps in poverty levels and wealth, educational achievements, incarceration numbers, etc., reflect the accumulation of inherited beliefs and practices about White superiority that have determined the social, economic, and political character of this nation.[1] Judith Butler has also noted that Whiteness in the U.S. has long been less a property of skin color than a social marker reproducing its dominant power in both explicit and implicit ways.[2]

So, racism is fundamentally a set of historical beliefs and practices that rest on existential claims about the higher intellectual, moral, and social virtues and values of White people in comparison to People of Color. It is my experience and contention that most of us continue to be infected, often unconsciously or naively, with some degree of this embedded racial hierarchy belief system. Moreover, many of our nation's public policies contain elements of White racial biases. So, unless we come to terms with our embedded White racial biases, the well-intended desire that many Whites are now expressing to be allied with People of Color in the fight against racial injustices will be performative at best. To become anti-racists, Whites must engage in the demanding work of dismantling our personal White racial biases and privileges that continue to stand as obstacles to creating the racial equity and justice we hope to achieve in America one day.

As I have listened to conversations about the frequency of racial events involving African Americans in recent years, I began to understand that White people often have trouble appreciating the differences in perceptions that non-Whites have about certain racial injustices. We might understand the anger, the distrust, and the unrelenting fear that the perpetual violence against People of Color elicits. At the same time, the engagement of my community in "courageous conversations" about race has produced some disturbing levels of White denial about the prevalence and persistence of racism and racial discrimination against People of Color.

I have been astonished by the number of educated and successful White people in my community who claim they do not make judgments about people based on skin color. Given the depth of feelings about race relations in America that so many of us have, it's difficult for me to imagine that we have escaped the legacy of White superiority that has permeated our social culture for generations on end. My experience tells me that most White people do notice visible racial identities and acknowledge these visible identities in our private conversations even while claiming to be "color blind." Most of us overlook the reality that we socially interact on a daily basis, primarily with those who share our racial identity, while pretending that racial integration is today's standard. It is telling that some of us say we are tired of hearing or talking about racism, particularly if the topic makes us feel guilty, ashamed, or anxious.

Even more troubling and counter-productive is the tendency among some of us to blame non-Whites for the social inequities or injustices that still exist. Wishing the issue would somehow go away may relieve us of the burden we sometimes feel when the subject of racism comes up. But this is a form of denial rather than a constructive confrontation with the issue. Consequently, I will explore how Whites sometimes attempt to avoid addressing the ideology of White superiority or White privilege instead of examining these roots of racism honestly and in a redemptive way. Even when Whites do recognize that we have been indoctrinated with some unconscious ideas about White racial superiority, there are few resources around to help us overcome our racial biases. I contend that it takes deliberate and dedicated effort to remove hierarchal ideas about racial identities. This is the allusive yet pressing challenge that I see confronting most of us who are White and want to become anti-racists.

Only individuals, of course, can decide to develop a deeper racial awareness in terms of how our "Whiteness" affects our relationships with People of Color. By calling this work a "confession," I include myself in the racism recovery process I am promoting in this book. So, I begin by offering my own racist confession to illustrate at a personal level how the ideology of White superiority and privilege can infect us without any intentional racial malice on our part. I also chose this descriptive title to signal the reader that

I see the process of overcoming racism as a spiritual issue for most of us. From a religious perspective, I believe that confessions serve an important function in bringing about reconciliation, particularly for broken relationships.

Moreover, my struggle with my acquired White racial biases has been inspired by a number of White people who found the emotional courage and intellectual integrity to admit they were implicated in the legacy of White racism in this country. Certainly, it takes a great deal of emotional and spiritual maturity and humility to admit our mistakes, to confront our misguided ideas, and to accept responsibility for our misbehavior rather than place blame on others for the alienation and distrust that has occurred in our relationships. When I enlarge this confessional attitude to include racial injustices that are entangled in America's past, it seems to me that White America has to own most of the responsibility for the sins of racism. If more of us can find the strength and courage to admit the racist sins of our past, I believe that racial reconciliation efforts will be advanced in ways that we have not yet been able to accomplish. My prayer is for us to remember the wisdom found in the spiritual and philosophical idea that the truth will set us free. So, I believe that racial reconciliation in America will move forward only as more White people can face the truth about how many of us have been shaped by racial biases that we have inherited, accepted, and perpetuated without examination or discussion across racial lines. In the words of James Baldwin, "Not everything that we face can be changed, but nothing can be changed until it is faced."

Confessing the accumulated sins of racism and our complicity in racial discrimination is not easy for White people, myself included. And all of us have our own unique experiences and struggles with racial biases. My wife, who was born and raised in Pittsburgh, Pennsylvania, has also realized how White racial biases were prevalent in the North, even though they were more subtle than what I experienced in the Deep South. As the reader will gather from my confessional narrative, racial awakenings occur in many different ways, some being gradual and some being more transformational than others. In my case, this White racist disease was so deeply ingrained that I will always have to consciously work at overcoming its influence. So, I call myself "a recovering racist" in the same way that recovering alcoholics speak of confronting and combating their substance abuse disease. As someone who identifies as being "White," I did not choose my skin color or create White racial biases. However, I do believe that I am responsible for dismantling the cultural racist indoctrination that I experienced in the early years of my life. I also believe that it is the collective responsibility of Whites in America to dismantle the racial biases and privileges that continue to persist in our culture and in our nation's institutions to this day. My confessional approach to becoming a recovering racist is meant to illustrate how White racial biases must be confronted and overcome at both personal and cultural levels. For me, this self-examination and reflection process has been racially freeing and a pathway to becoming an anti-racist. My hope is that this kind of examination and confession of White racial biases may do the same for others.

CHAPTER ONE
CONFESSING MY INHERITED RACIAL BIASES

"A year never goes by, indeed, in which I cannot look back and see in my conduct or concepts some vestiges of White racism. Old poisons run deep."

—Larry L. King, *Confessions of a White Racist*

As the title of this book suggests, I identify myself as a "recovering racist." What I mean by this identification is that my personal history has been steeped in White racial biases and identity from which I have had to work throughout my adult life to free myself. This self-identification also acknowledges that my developmental journey to overcome overt forms of racism has been a slow process filled with many revelatory experiences and turning points. My recovery from the explicit forms of racism is certainly not unique. Many White people today realize that we live in a racist nation where it is difficult for us to be exempt from some amount of old White racial biases and privileges. Nevertheless, many of us like to believe we have shed the most egregious White-skin prejudices of the past and no longer embrace the worse forms of overt racism. My personal confession will certainly support this contention. What I ask the reader to look for in this account of my confessional history is what persistent attitude or racial bias seems to have shaped my struggle for freedom from racism. Every one of us has our own story and personal experiences with racial biases, whether these are large or small. What I am hoping my history might reveal to the reader is the underlying root cause of White racism.

Looking back over my history, I can see now how my White racist indoctrination was carried out in my family of origin. My parents had acquired White racism from their upbringing in Georgia and South Carolina when Jim Crow era attitudes were very much in place. Upon my birth in 1947, I was raised in a rural White community outside the city of Jacksonville, Florida. I learned implicitly as a child that White people were somehow better than the Black people who were segregated off in the "Colored sections" of Jacksonville, far away from our neighborhood. Isolated in a White community away from Black folks, one of my earliest recollections about "Colored people" (the polite euphemism used during those days to refer to African Americans) was from my encounters with Gus and Pearl McNair. The McNairs were an aging husband and wife who lived in what appeared to be a dilapidated old house sitting on the side of U.S. Highway 17, several miles north of our neighborhood. Gus was a small Black man in his eighties who walked with a slight limp and looked like he had worked too long and too hard over his many years. I only came to know Gus because he did odd jobs in our neighborhood, mowing lawns, trimming trees, and providing cheap manual labor for White folks who needed help on occasion. His wife, Pearl, provided housekeeping services for some of the families in our neighborhood, including my aunt, who lived next door.

From this limited exposure to one African American family, I came to believe that Black people, on the whole, were poor, uneducated, and submissive to and dependent on White people for employment and charity. This stereotype of African Americans was reinforced by our travels into the city when we would pass through "nigger town" with row after row of unpainted and deteriorating shot-gun houses with Black men sitting on old sofas on the front porches. The popular White myth was that these people were lazy and satisfied with living in relative poverty. The ideology of White superiority was institutionalized in our government buildings, businesses, schools, banks, and restaurants where Black people worked menial jobs as janitors, laborers, and wait staff but could not sit and eat together with White people. Black people even conformed to this idea of White superiority by always speaking to White people with a subservient tone of "yes, sir" or "no, ma'am," and never saying anything that might call attention to themselves.

I became aware of the racial tensions that occurred during the early years of the civil rights movement when a few younger Black people in Jacksonville asserted their resistance to White racism and injustices. On the whole, my parents were passive racists and did not exhibit the kind of hatred or fear of Black people that some other White people were expressing at that time. Around the age of eleven or twelve, I remember riding in our family car and noticing a KKK rally taking place on a vacant field not far from where I went to school. As we drove by slowly, I saw a large assembly of people in white-hooded outfits gathered around a bonfire. They were listening to a speech from one of their leaders who was standing on a makeshift wooden platform. In the center of the crowd, I noticed there was a Black-faced mannequin hanging from a rope with a noose around its neck near the fire. Intrigued by this unusual and ominous spectacle, I asked my dad what was going on. He kept looking ahead as he drove by slowly, saying rather sternly, "You don't want to have anything to do with them."

This was the first time I can remember thinking that some White racial prejudices must be wrong, and "colored" people were sometimes the targets of an unexplained White hatred. Part of the message I absorbed from this disturbing experience was that some aspects of White racism had a very ugly face to it. I also learned that we would not talk about this brand of viral racism for some undeclared reason within our polite White community.

Our racially segregated Southern culture of the 1950s and 1960s also legitimized White superiority in ways that were rarely questioned. To avoid any close contact with African Americans, even the public beaches at our local Talbot Island State Park were segregated. In this social context, the White mythology about Black people appeared to be supported by the realities I observed in the world around me and in the narratives told by White people about People of Color. Our racially segregated schools at the time prevented us from having any firsthand contact with Black people.

One of my first recollections about Black kids occurred for me when my school's patrol unit from my suburban junior high school participated in a parade in downtown Jacksonville. I recall being fascinated by the Black high school band that was playing and marching in the parade that day immediately in front of our group. The energetic rhythms of the drums and horns that produced the music of this Black marching band were mesmerizing to me. I was fascinated as well by their striking White uniforms with boldly colored blue and gold hats. But, even then, African Americans just seemed like exotic people who were somehow culturally different from those of us who were White. As captivating as the performance of this marching band was for me, it was common for White adults to say this was "jungle music" with overly emotional and physical characteristics not fitting for civilized people. Even though I liked the African American style of music, I was expected to honor the perspective of my White elders about Black people and their ways.

My first real personal experience with a Black person came from a friendship I developed with a young Black man named Willie during the summer months when I was out of school. After World War II, my father worked for a regional insurance company headquartered in downtown Jacksonville, where he became the supply department manager. Willie worked in my dad's department, filling supply orders that were shipped out to offices around the Southeast. As the boss's son, I could go down into the basement of the office building where Willie worked and hang out with him as he went about his daily job. Willie always seemed pleased when I would show up, and I felt useful and entertained at the same time by our friendly banter and his willingness to let me help pull supplies from the shelves. From those summertime conversations, I learned that Willie and I had many of the same thoughts and feelings about things that happened in life, even though he was more than fifteen years older than me.

Through this personal relationship with a Black man, some of my racist ideas and the White stereotyping I had learned about "colored people" began to fade. From our weekly interactions during the summer months, I came to appreciate that Willie was a person like me who had feelings, wants, and needs and a good measure of humor. Consequently, some of my racist stereotypes about lazy, ignorant Black people were quickly demystified. I began to think of Willie as an older friend with whom I enjoyed hanging out whenever I went to my dad's office. For whatever reason, it did not seem to bother my dad that I wanted to head off as soon as we got to his office to spend most of the day with Willie.

After a couple of summers, I had almost forgotten that Willie was a "Colored" man. One day, while visiting with Willie in his workspace, he reminded me that it was near noontime, and my dad would be waiting for me to come to his upstairs office for us to go to lunch. Willie always had a lunch sack, and he would go to the restroom to wash up before he sat in the basement to eat his sandwich. That particular day, I happened to be engaged in a lengthy conversation with Willie when I unwittingly followed him into the "Colored" restroom in the basement. When Willie realized that I had followed him into the restroom, he turned around with a look of horror on his face and insisted that I leave immediately. I was perplexed by Willie's reaction. To me, that restroom looked exactly like the restroom for Whites. But Willie kept pointing me to the door, saying with some urgency that I needed to leave. When I exited the colored restroom, a hand suddenly grabbed me by the neck, pushing me up against the wall. It was my dad who had come looking for me to go to lunch. My dad said to me in an angry tone, "If I ever catch you in that restroom again, I'll beat you until you can't walk."

I was shocked by my dad's threat, and I realized that I had momentarily forgotten to respect the color line that separated me from Willie. While I had not created this White and Black social demarcation, I learned that day how deeply ingrained it was in our society. This frightening experience made it clear how important it was for me to obey this racial separation between Whites and Blacks. These socially imposed racial barriers were not open for me to change based on my personal feelings about People of Color. I also became sensitized that day to how racist Whites often use fear and intimidation to keep other Whites from questioning the color line code.

One of the pivotable times when I began to question White attitudes about Black people took place one Sunday after church when all my aunts and uncles and cousins were together for dinner at our house. The Sunday custom in my extended family was for all the Snead clan to gather at one of our homes in the neighborhood for a family-style meal after church services. The men would sit in the living room with the television on to watch a ball game while the women arranged the tables with the various dishes that my aunts had made and brought over for the meal. When the meal was ready, we were all called to the tables. After saying grace, the bowls of vegetables and platters of roast beef or fried chicken would be passed around while lively family conversations were taking place. The TV was left on during the meal so the men in the family could keep up with the score of the game.

On this memorable Sunday, as we were eating dinner together, the TV broadcast of the ball game was interrupted by a special news report. We all stopped and watched the report about civil rights marchers somewhere in Alabama led by a Black man in a suit who made a speech. I didn't pay much attention to what was being said in the news report. But, as soon as the ball game resumed and the adults went back to talking, one of my uncles said plainly, "Someone ought to kill that nigger!" as he passed a bowl of peas around the table. The force of that statement condoning racial violence struck me as a massive violation of the Sunday School lesson I had just heard at church earlier in the day about our calling in Jesus' name to love our neighbors. *That was the day I dropped out of going to church because of the hypocrisy I heard coming from a family member who claimed to be a devout Christian.* At that moment, I could not escape the realization that I was part of a racist family. The religious and moral contradictions I felt that Sunday had a profound impact on my self-understanding of White racism and how this was contributing to the social upheaval going on around the South at that time. However, I knew full well not to question the White racial standards that gave rise to this racist comment.

My first recollection of feeling shame about the destructiveness of White racism did not occur until I was in high school. Most of us teenagers had come to think that the segregated schools in Jacksonville reflected a cultural belief about the intellectual inferiority of Black people. The small rural community in which I lived outside the city limits required us to take a school bus to the nearest high school in the city. The other option was for us to ride to school in a car with our older high school friends who had a driver's license. So, most days, I would hitch a ride to school with one of my friends. One morning as we were headed to school, the driver of the car and my cousin, who was sitting up front with him, noticed an African American teenager walking on the sidewalk going in the same direction we were traveling. We all knew he wasn't going to our school. It had rained earlier that morning, so the roads were still wet. Pointing to this Black kid walking along on the sidewalk, my cousin said, "Let's get him!"

Peering from the back seat of the car, I noticed the driver swerving close to the sidewalk as we passed by the Black kid. There was a large puddle of rainwater in the right lane next to the curb, and the car hit the puddle so that it splashed the Black kid and soaked him. I can still remember the laughter that erupted from the front seat of the car from this dastardly act against an unsuspecting and innocent Black kid. I recall turning around in my seat in the car and looking out the back windshield to see this kid holding his head down with his dripping arms by his side, apparently in shock and humiliation at being splashed by our car. This despicable racist act somehow struck my moral sensibilities with feelings of sadness, regret, shame, and guilt. Yet, I alone seemed to feel bad about what we did because the others in the car were celebrating with racist glee. I said nothing at that moment, but this vicious act of racism made me deeply aware that Black people were considered by many White people to be less than human, deserving no respect. I knew what we had done to this Black kid simply wasn't right by any moral standard, and I realized at that moment I was implicated as a passenger in the car in this act of White racism.

It wasn't until later in high school, however, that I experienced the full force of this cultural racism that caused me to seriously rethink what I had been taught about "the races." My history teacher pointed out in class one day that "Sunday mornings were among the most segregated times in American society," noting the irony of how a predominately "Christian culture" kept things that way.

Up to that time, I had never questioned the societal structures within which I lived. While the civil rights movement was certainly taking place at the time, for the most part, we were isolated as White kids from the racial strife erupting around the South. I don't recall my history teacher directly challenging the idea of White racial superiority that existed at that time. But the obvious truth of my teacher's social and racial observations began to gnaw at my assumptions about the Christian calling to love our neighbors that I repeatedly heard every Sunday at the small Baptist church my family and all my relatives attended regularly. It dawned on me that all the Baptist churches I had ever come across in the rural parts of the county where we lived didn't have any People of Color in them. Once again, the contradictions between what was being preached and taught in my church about Jesus' love and the derogatory things I often heard from my family and friends about Black people began to seep slowly into my otherwise narrow moral and religious White consciousness. The recognition of this racist social structure by my high school teacher with the suggestion that this racial segregation violated our nation's stated principles made me question, even more, some of the racist notions I had acquired from my family and our White culture.

Unlike most of my childhood friends, I went off to college in 1966 and discovered a world decidedly different from the overtly racist world of my younger years. This educational exposure, along with my introduction to the Presbyterian church, greatly expanded my worldview. I began to suspect that I had been duped by some of the narrow social values I had been taught as a child. In my early adult years returning home from college, I found myself wondering how a Black man, like Gus, really felt about living in that part of Florida as a "Colored" person. Gus had lived his entire life in a cultural atmosphere of southern racism that I knew full well had existed for generations in that part of North Florida. Surely, I thought, Gus must have experienced a great deal of racial discrimination during his lifetime in that community.

I was acutely aware that all the White people made it plain and clear to Gus and Pearl that they were "colored people," and that fact alone made them somehow less socially respectable. Even when the "White" and "Colored" restroom and water-fountain signs had been taken down from all public buildings in Jacksonville, it was evident that White racism still existed. Despite the impact of the civil rights movement elsewhere, racial prejudice continued to shape the hearts and minds of most White folks in our rural working-class community.

It seemed that Gus had developed his deferential demeanor from years of living around White people who made every African American very aware of the sharp color line that divided the races in the South since the days of slavery. So, in my periodic conversations with Gus, I tried to indicate to him privately my recognition of my family's racist views and to sympathize with him about the prevalence of racism in which he had to live. Gus always seemed uncomfortable when I tried to engage him in these conversations. When I discussed this issue with a Presbyterian minister friend, he suggested that Gus may have learned to keep to himself how he felt about the social barriers he lived under simply as a matter of survival. Trusting his wisdom, I accepted this explanation and became more sensitized to the plight of People of Color who had been marginalized and oppressed by the dominant White social values and attitudes under which we all lived. As I had learned from my experience with my dad, there were severe consequences for anyone who challenged the White racist system. Moreover, I lived in a largely suburban White world segregated away from People of Color in the city. During these years, I was oblivious to the racial tensions taking place in Jacksonville when the "Axe-handle Saturday" event had occurred downtown in 1960. Looking back on my experiences in high school and college years, I now see that I represented those who Dr. Martin Luther King, Jr. pointed to in his 1968 sermon at the National Cathedral, suggesting many Whites were "sleeping through a revolution."

Up until leaving home for college and meeting more People of Color, there were not many opportunities for me to question the cultural racism that characterized most White communities at that time. By attending segregated public schools, there was never an opportunity to talk honestly with a Black peer about racial issues or to question the White stereotypes about Black people in general. That quickly changed for me when a military draft notice showed up in my mailbox as I started to attend college. After dropping out after one semester in college, my military deferment was removed. Suddenly, the likelihood of being drafted for service during the Vietnam war became a real concern. Thanks to my dad's social connections, I was allowed to join the Army National Guard in Florida.

It was during my Army basic training at Fort Benning, Georgia, that I had another eye-opening opportunity to confront the White racism I had been immersed in as a child. My basic training company had an African American drill instructor who made it plain to us that his goal was to teach us how to survive the combat duty we were being prepared for in Vietnam. Since the majority of us in my company were White, I was impressed with his care and concern for our well-being even as he ran us ragged with physical exercises. My attitudes about Black people were also dramatically changed by a number of the other would-be soldiers who were there with me in basic training. To avoid the draft, a number of the star players with the Atlanta Falcons football team had joined the National Guard and were also sent to Ft. Benning for basic training. To my surprise, these young Black men in my platoon were not only in extremely good physical condition, but they were also well educated, intelligent, and economically very well off.

My platoon leader in basic training was Junior Coffee, a star running back for the Falcons at that time. In short order, I found myself looking up to these Black athletes who were part of my army training experience. Once again, my personal encounters with People of Color led me to rethink the racial rules of the White society I had lived in. This experience in the army added to my embarrassment and resentment about the racist attitudes that had been part of my childhood indoctrination. My appreciation for these African American professional athletes led me to distrust and even resent many of the White racial stereotypes and biases that were held by my family of origin and my southern culture.

My increasing awareness about the racial dynamics of the late 1960s took another step when I returned to college and found a part-time delivery job for an office supply company in Jacksonville. I was assigned to work in the afternoons with Herbert, a Black man in his early forties. Herbert was a long-time employee of the company who worked in the warehouse filling office supply orders. Because he was friendly and outgoing, I learned that Herbert had grown up in the poor inner city of Jacksonville and had stayed in this low-paying job in order to support his family. However, he was amazingly vocal with me about his belief that his skin color contributed to his minimum wage job and his limitations as a Person of Color working for this company. His honest commentaries about racial prejudices and the dynamics of White privilege were revealing, insightful, and sad to me. Herbert's ability to express his racial awareness stood in stark contrast to the often-unmentioned racism that existed in our White culture. He was candid about how he saw the color line functioning all around us, and my conversations with him gave me a deeper understanding of how a Black person experienced and felt about White racism.

Herbert was also the first person I can remember suggesting that racism was tied directly to the lack of economic opportunities, the scarcity of accumulated wealth, and sub-standard education that African Americans had experienced for generations. While Herbert wasn't militant at that time regarding White racism, he certainly made the point, from his experience as a Black man, that White people weren't going to change their racist attitudes easily. He took pains to point out how the power of money dictated the social rules under which we live. The truth of Herbert's perspective about White racism and economic inequalities has been borne out for me repeatedly over the past fifty years. Working with Herbert impressed upon me the critical importance of White people having opportunities to listen to the experiences of People of Color before we make any claims about understanding racism.

By the time I had finished college, confronting White racism within my family was almost as hard as confronting my own racism. I knew full well, for instance, that my mother saw distinct racial differences between herself as a White woman and Gus as a Black man. This racial difference was always front and center for her. As I came to appreciate the African American struggle against racism, I was often embarrassed and bothered by how my mother talked to Gus as though he was a second-class person. As a clear statement about the differences she saw between the races, my mother kept an old drinking glass turned upside down on a spigot outside the house for Gus to use whenever he came to work for her and wanted a drink of water. It irritated me that my mother would always pay Gus less for his labor than she would pay any of the White teenage boys who mowed her grass or did other household chores for her.

Occasionally, when she had an old appliance or vacuum that had quit working, she would ask Gus if he wanted it instead of putting it into the trash. To her way of thinking, a defective item would be a nice gift for any colored person who was poor. Sadly enough, Gus would oblige my mother's White superiority by taking the hand-me-down "gift" that would otherwise get junked. To make matters worse, at least in my mind, Gus would always thank my mother for these pitiful tokens of generosity. While both Gus and my mother accepted without question the racial barriers and codes of their generation, this racist conditioning did not make it right in my mind. Nevertheless, I was unsure about how I could challenge that kind of White racism embedded in my mother or other family members.

Thankfully, while in college, I met a young woman named Rosie, who raised my racial consciousness in some profound yet unexpected ways. As a college student, she lived next door to where I worked in the afternoons, and she worked part-time for a non-denominational Christian youth organization in Jacksonville that was addressing racial issues among teenagers in the inner city. It was through dating her and getting involved with the Young Life program that my awareness of racial issues was significantly expanded.

When I first asked Rosie for a date, she informed me that she was moving from the more affluent part of Jacksonville, where she had been raised to an old inner-city neighborhood that had become racially mixed and in decline. For a moment, I considered backing out on a date with her when she told me she was moving to the Springfield section of town to live in an apartment above an African American funeral home. She proudly shared with me that she was going to live there as a White person to work with the Young Life program aimed at helping White and Black teenagers get beyond their racial distrust and conflicts with one another. Over the next few months, I became more and more impressed with her sense of compassion for young people, regardless of their race, most of whom in that part of the city were marginalized by poverty.

She also introduced me to a Presbyterian minister who was unafraid to challenge many of the cultural and religious biases that had created and maintained the racial and economic barriers in the community. From this exposure, I found myself gravitating toward a new social awareness that was more compatible with my earlier Christian beliefs about the power of love and Jesus' concern for the marginalized.

Fortunately, I had the good sense to marry Rosie, and with her help, I found a direction for my life that led me to pursue a vocational ministry in the Presbyterian church. Ironically, the southern denominational branch of the Presbyterian church had split off from the "northern" Presbyterian church at the outset of the Civil War over the issue of slavery and White supremacy. However, my awareness of the institutional aspects of White racism had not been developed at that time.

Rosie's innate impatience with White racism showed up forcefully for me a few years after we were married. While attending graduate school at Florida State University in Tallahassee in the early 1970s, we made it a practice to go back to Jacksonville frequently so our daughter could spend time with her grandparents. My father had died, and my mother would ask me on these periodic visits to make repairs to her house. On one occasion, she asked me to address a chronic problem she was having with the septic system in the backyard. She knew that the septic tank drain field lines would need to be dug up and replaced. So, my mother indicated she would hire Gus to help me dig up the old drain lines and install new drainpipes when I came over.

The morning we were to begin the work, Gus and I greeted each other with our usual pleasantries and started excavating the old drain line. After an hour or so, my mother came to the back porch and asked if we wanted some ice water or tea. I responded by saying we would appreciate a cold drink. In a few minutes, my mother came out carrying a tray with a pitcher of ice water and a glass filled with ice. At that point, she said to Gus, "Your glass is over there," pointing to the old glass turned upside down on the faucet at the back of the house. It was clear to me at that moment that I needed to confront my mother's racism, but I stood there momentarily frozen, trying to figure out how to address this racist comment without condemning her.

Before I said anything, Rosie came rushing out the back door of the house asking Gus to wait a minute before he got his "glass." I was surprised she had noticed that my mother filled only one glass with ice, so Rosie immediately went to my mother's China cabinet and took out one of her fine crystal glasses and had quickly filled it with ice and rushed outside, saying, "Here, Gus, this is for you."

As she handed him the glass of ice with a smile, she poured him some water from the pitcher my mother was still holding on the tray. Gus looked at me uneasily, and I simply said, "Enjoy a glass of cold water, Gus." My mother never said a word as Gus thanked my wife, and she went back into the house, quietly seething at my mother's racist action. As for me, I experienced that day a needed measure of strength from my wife to take a stand that I had previously been reluctant to take when cultural White racism would raise its ugly head. This experience revealed to me that I did not have the courage it takes for White people to confront instances of White racial biases that others close to us might express.

By the time I had entered graduate school at Florida State University in 1973, the civil rights movement, along with African American students and athletes affirming Black Power, had challenged a lot of the overt racism that characterized so much of our White southern culture. Slowly, I began to recognize the broader reaches of racism that had completely escaped me because of my own racial biases. At that time, Florida State University had only a few African American students. Most Black students who went to a state college attended Florida A&M University, an institution of higher education in Tallahassee created for African American students at the end of the nineteenth century. Even though integration had already occurred in these two state universities, the old racial divide was still obvious in terms of who went to which school.

To finance my studies at FSU, I took a job driving a school bus for a fundamentalist Christian school in town. I soon learned that this private White school had been established to circumvent school desegregation in the 1960s. I also discovered that most of the African Americans lived in the "French town" section of Tallahassee. When I took an additional part-time job in the kitchen of a chain seafood restaurant, I started working with three or four African American students who were employed there as well. There was, at that time, a subtle but clear social separation among us as Black and White workers, and we joked openly about our racial differences. On several occasions, it became apparent to me that the young African American men working among us did not trust the White restaurant management to treat them in the same way the White employees were treated. I became sympathetic to their complaints about subtle racial bias because I could see how White identity functioned as a kind of social bonding dynamic for some of us while isolating People of Color. At first, I thought this socially isolating behavior originated with the pride and distrust of our Black co-workers. But, over time, I realized that there was an institutional preference and favoritism toward those of us who were White. The restaurant manager would always give the Black workers a hard time about being a few minutes late to work while ignoring the same kind of tardiness among those of us who were White. It also became more evident to me from this mixed-race work experience how economic, social, and political power structures impact People of Color while providing me and other White people with certain benefits not extended to non-Whites. As I remember it, the restaurant manager would warn the Black workers about "stealing" food while allowing the White workers to take home any remaining seafood that had been cooked and not sold at the end of the day. These subtle differences forced me to appreciate the suspicion and resentments that many Black people at that time had about anyone who was White. Nevertheless, none of us Whites were willing to openly challenge the racial inequities we noticed in our workplace, so I was like the others who over-looked the racism that was in our midst.

My graduate school education and Presbyterian church experi-ence in Tallahassee reinforced my gradual racial awakening and my wider understanding of ministry in the church. I learned in my re-ligion classes at FSU about "the social gospel movement" at the be-ginning of the twentieth century and the efforts to directly link the "Fatherhood of God" to the "Brotherhood of Man," which had been unknown to me in my Christian experience up to that time. With the encouragement of the professor who was guiding my master's thesis, I decided in 1975 to attend seminary at Colgate Rochester

Divinity School in Rochester, New York. In addition to the theological liberation from conservative brands of Christianity that I found in this divinity school, my seminary experience also enlarged my racial awareness and exposed me to the events and elements in the civil rights movement that I had slept through in large measure.

Several years before my arrival at the divinity school, a merger had occurred between Colgate Rochester, Bexley Hall, and Crozer Seminaries. I discovered that Martin Luther King, Jr. had graduated from Crozer Seminary when it was located near Philadelphia. Consequently, a pipeline of African American students, many of whom were from the South, had been established at Crozer Seminary. So, when I arrived at the merged divinity schools, nearly half of the student body was African American. While we attended classes together, the campus was still racially segregated socially, with the African American students keeping to themselves. We heard stories about how a previous generation of African American students had locked the administration building in protest against academic indifference to issues impacting Blacks around the country. Both the Black students and the Black faculty made it clear to us that the Black church and Black theology were decidedly different from the White versions of liberal Christianity at the time.

Freedom from oppression, in the form of White racism, was a common theme that shaped the understanding of Black theology. I learned about not only the role that African American churches played in the civil rights movement of the 1960s but also an awareness that many African Americans would no longer be defined by the theological, social, or political mindset of White people.

Black power was being affirmed, and White institutional power was being challenged. This seminary experience contributed significantly to my ongoing racial awareness awakening. I came away from seminary with two abiding notions about White racism: First, that conservative Christianity tended to place individual ethics above social ethics, so social sins like racism could be easily ignored. Secondly, White society and most White churches had a spiritual aversion to addressing racism, particularly if doing so would require a transformation of our White privileges or challenge our identity as being among the "good" people on the planet. Regrettably, it would be years later before I would associate this "spiritual aversion" to addressing racism with our inherited attachment to our biases about White superiority. By the time I graduated from seminary, my field education experiences in several churches had encouraged me to pursue a call to serve as a church pastor, assuming I could find a church liberal enough theologically to call me.

Fortunately, I received a call to serve as the pastor of a small Presbyterian church in the Tidewater area of Virginia in 1978. Returning to the South, my racial awakening was quickly stultified by my immersion into a predominantly White mainline denomination in a White suburban community. All the members of my congregation were White, and we lived in a White neighborhood outside the city of Portsmouth. The only occasion I had to think about racial issues during the three years I served that church came about when I was involved with a campus ministry at a local community college. A group of pastors in the area were invited to develop a campus ministry for the commuter students who attended the college. We decided early on to identify ways we could engage the students while they were on campus around spiritual issues and raise awareness about our presence on campus as well.

As we considered how we might reach the students, a young female African American pastor created a stir among our ministerial group when she suggested we hold a student forum on the topic of race relations. Her idea was simple. She proposed that we reserve a room on campus and put signs up with a date and time for students and faculty to come to address the topic "Black is Right, White is Wrong." While I agreed with her bold suggestion that this would certainly get the kind of attention our campus ministry team wanted to create, most of the White ministers and the faculty were extremely nervous about this suggestion. It was a troubling discovery for me to realize that the predominately White religious and institutional leaders were not willing to address racial issues even at the time when race riots were occurring in various parts of America. Just talking about Black/White issues was too scary and too "controversial" for pastors of established White churches to address.

This experience made me aware of how difficult it is for us as White people to question racism when we fear our White identity might be challenged. I was unwilling, however, to speak up about the White fear because I wanted to be accepted by the dominant and older White ministers involved in this ministry. This desire to avoid controversy and stay in good standing within church circles became the excuse I used not to raise racial issues I knew were going on around us at that time.

In 1982 I accepted the call to become the associate pastor of a larger White Presbyterian church in an affluent suburb of Dallas, Texas. During this experience, my awareness of race issues continued to be a latent aspect of my ministry. White racism was rarely mentioned within our White congregation or our Presbyterian connections. Only twice in my eight years of service with that church do I remember a discussion of race issues ever coming up.

One was when a group of churches in North Dallas came together to create a cooperative ministry to help people in need in the city. Initially, all the representatives from the twenty-plus churches thought it would be great for us to pool our resources to create a food pantry and to assist clients living in poverty with paying their rent and utility bills. Large amounts of money and volunteer help poured in from the affluent churches in North Dallas to provide charitable help for people living in poverty who were largely People of Color. As we discussed the guidelines for this charitable ministry, some of the church leaders suggested that we limit the amounts of funding for rent and utility assistance because they argued we would be promoting a "welfare" attitude among the African Americans and Latino folks who came looking for help. As the guideline discussions continued, I learned that White affluent church folks who thought of themselves as compassionate people tended to think that People of Color were inherently lazy and needed to be held responsible for living in and getting out of poverty. Any suggestion that this attitude sounded like a mild version of paternalistic racism was met with considerable objection and resentment. This experience taught me that White denial about our racist views runs deep. But, once again, I didn't have the moral courage to challenge the implicit racial biases there were expressed in this context.

After this shared ministry effort was well established, we hired a young Presbyterian minister to serve as the director of the program primarily because he had a social work background. He soon proposed that our shared ministry should identify a few clients who would receive more comprehensive help to get them out of the cycle of poverty through job training, childcare assistance, and a whole range of long-term financial and personal support. When the board of the shared ministry rejected this approach, I was struck by his comment that most affluent White churches are more interested in providing charity than working to establish social justice.

This same criticism, with its racial implications, was later amplified for me when the senior pastor of our church invited an African American minister to come to preach at one of our Sunday worship services. A furor erupted in our congregation when this African American jail chaplain suggested in his sermon that most established mainline churches in predominately White denominations conveniently ignore racial justice issues in the criminal justice system. Both of these experiences in Dallas made me cognizant of what I now call "White resistance"—the idea that White people are heavily invested in maintaining White power systems and White morality issues. It seems that our White denial about racial discrimination is pervasive among those of us who live in predominantly White suburbs and have little direct contact with People of Color. Without any real familiarity with People of Color, I discovered it is easy for me and our congregation to maintain a level of ignorance and denial about the reaches of systemic racism.

My next racial awakening came with a move to Houston in 1988 to serve as the pastor of a church in the southwestern part of the city. While the church's surrounding community had originally reflected an upper-middle-class history for several decades, there were clear indications by then that this church was in a changing neighborhood, being impacted by what was called "White flight." Upwardly mobile African Americans had started to buy relatively nice homes in the Southwest corner of the city where the church was located. In just a few years, the fear of declining property values from this influx of People of Color created a domino effect with many White people selling their homes and moving out to the newer White suburbs. Shortly after arriving at this church, a growing number of our church members would let me know they were reluctantly moving out of the neighborhood and would be joining a church closer to their new home. It never occurred to me that I should sell my home in that area out of the perceived fear of a more diverse community. The heavy Jewish population in the area made it known that they would not abandon that area of the city. As an open-minded pastor, I was encouraged when a few African Americans and interracial families began to visit and then join our church. After a few years of declining membership, however, it was evident that we now had a smaller predominantly White congregation housed in a facility designed for a congregation twice our current size. Again, I focused my attention on the survival of my church rather than on addressing the White fear issues creating the changing neighborhood.

After a couple of years contending with the reality of our changing neighborhood, I heard a report at a Presbytery meeting about the problems a small African American congregation in South Houston was facing with their aging facilities. The African American pastor of this church happened to mention to me that he had recently bought a home near my church. In a moment of inspiration, I came up with the idea that our two congregations could share our expansive church facilities. This made perfect sense to me. Their small congregation would not have to try to raise large amounts of money to repair a deteriorating church building, and our church would benefit from having another congregation sharing in our operational expenses. So, I invited the pastor of this African American congregation to have lunch with me to talk about this idea I had developed. Our denomination at that time was encouraging churches in changing neighborhoods to look for creative ways to engage the diversity issues often involved in these "transitions in ministry." For once, I thought, *I am on the cutting edge of promoting both creative urban ministry and a bold way to address social justice issues.*

When the African American pastor embraced my idea enthusiastically, we made arrangements for the leadership of our two congregations to have a meeting to discuss together the possibility of sharing one church facility. The pastor and I even fantasized about our two congregations eventually merging so we would have one of the few interracial Presbyterian churches in the state, if not in the South. We also scheduled a meeting with our Presbytery executive to get his thoughts on some of the legal or administrative issues we might face in pursuing this idea. To our delight, he too was enthusiastic about this idea.

Together, the three of us outlined a tentative process by which to explore the merits of this idea with our congregations and the issues we would need to address—scheduling worship services on Sunday mornings to accommodate the two congregations, sharing other parts of the facility for office space and educational classes, planning periodic combined worship services and fellowship dinners, etc. I was very encouraged when our two leadership groups from our respective congregations embraced this idea of sharing ministry space and working together as a progressive Presbyterian witness in our racially changing neighborhood. In a matter of months, we had developed a shared ministry agreement and were enjoying this interracial church experiment, or so I thought. The first troubling issue I sought to downplay rather than address honestly was around the issue some of my church members raised about who might eventually become the pastor of the church if our two congregations might be merged into one. In short, I ignored the comments that most of my congregation made about not wanting a Black pastor.

About six months into this adventure, I received a call one Sunday evening from the pastor of the African American congregation asking for my help. He was trying to lead a prayer service in the fellowship hall at the church when one of my lay leaders was in the kitchen banging pans and disrupting their prayer time. He had tried to ask this White female member of our church to respect their presence in the fellowship hall, but he claimed she was rude and uncooperative. So, I drove down to the church and confronted my church member about her disruptive behavior. When I asked her what she was doing, she expressed aggravation that "they" were in the fellowship hall at the time she had planned to set up the room for a Girl Scouts meeting she wanted to have that evening. After pointing out that our partner congregation had scheduled their service on the master calendar to use this space, she only became more defensive about "our" church's priority for using the facilities.

When I tried to indicate that our African American friends had every right to utilize this space per our agreements, she complained more vocally, saying, "I knew those people would try to take over our church, and you have let them do it." She then turned and walked out, muttering something about Blacks taking advantage of goodhearted White people. I was embarrassed and angry about her behavior and the comments this White woman in my church was making about our African American brothers and sisters. So, I apologized to the pastor and indicated that I would call a leadership meeting of our church to address this issue.

To my surprise and great disappointment, my church's all-White leadership group generally backed the perceptions of this unhappy member that our African American friends were "abusing our welcome" to help them by sharing our church facilities with them. These lay leaders in my church were now telling me that they resented the way that the African American pastor and I had pushed this shared ministry idea on them. Some were arguing that the African American congregation was not paying their fair share of the rent, and all we were doing was encouraging more People of Color to move into our otherwise decent neighborhood. I left the meeting that night spiritually disillusioned and went home and told my wife that I was going to resign my position as pastor of the church because of the racist attitudes that had surfaced in this meeting. This experience in my church pushed me to see even more contradictions between the values we were professing in Christ's name, and the realities of racism that I had been willing to accept or overlook for years before. I simply found it difficult to tolerate this kind of open racism.

So, out of frustration with that church experience in Houston, I decided to look for another pastoral call in a more open-minded congregation. Looking back on this experience, I now realize my lack of tolerance for addressing deep-seated racial issues with members of my congregation was in part my unwillingness to address my own embedded and embarrassing racial biases.

Thankfully, in 1995, I received a call from a progressive Presbyterian church in Austin, Texas, to serve as their pastor. This church had a history of ministry in the community with marginalized people, so it was a good match for me in terms of both my theological development and the kind of social justice ministry they and I wanted to express. One of the blessings I discovered in my ministry in Austin was the relationship I formed with Mike, an African American who had worked for years in the county health and human services department, trying to assist struggling people in the community with their basic needs. As a native of Austin, Mike was acutely aware of how race played a significant role in the development of this city. He was quick to point out that Austin had been racially segregated for years and divided economically by the interstate highway running through its center. When it came to dealing with racism, Mike challenged, often with humor and irony, the popular White perceptions about the city being a forward-thinking and progressive community. I came to appreciate Mike's willingness to talk honestly and with a sense of humor about the racial issues he saw at work all around us. In time, I discovered he was using his community connections to bring people together to talk about advancing racial harmony in the city.

Somewhere between the candid conversations that Mike and I had about race matters and the community organizing efforts I was involved in, I began to realize how the use of institutional power contributes to maintaining racial inequities and biases. Without hearing the perspectives of People of Color, I began to doubt that White people can fully understand or appreciate how institutional power impacts our perceptions and attitudes about race. Mike helped me to see that Austin was divided along historic racial lines and by issues related to maintaining White political power and control. He suggested that this long-standing racial segregation in the city kept White people from noticing the poverty and urban problems that the People of Color on the east side were experiencing while Austin was otherwise booming economically. Conversations within the White community made it clear to everyone that the East side of Austin was the poor area where racial minorities just happened to live even while gentrification was taking place in that part of town. Like many other Whites, I concluded this racial divide existed more as an economic issue rather than as a residual from historic White racial biases. In retrospect, it was easier for my congregation and me to attribute the nagging racial disparities we saw around us to wealth and employment issues rather than to White racial biases and institutional practices.

I remember our church studying appreciatively the poignant letter Dr. Martin Luther King, Jr. wrote in 1963 from the Birmingham jail to White church leaders about racial justice issues in their city, yet never bothering to ask ourselves how our racial biases and White privileges impacted People of Color in our own community.

Over the seventeen years that I served as the pastor of this near inner-city church, my awareness of the racial divide between Whites, Browns, and Blacks in Austin was constantly before us. During this time, there were police shootings of unarmed African American and Latino men in the city that generated momentary concerns about racial justice issues. Meanwhile, the gentrification of predominantly minority communities in the city was taking place, and the public schools were reflecting troubling gaps in educational achievements along racial lines.

My involvement in the local community organizing effort reinforced my understanding of the resistance of the dominant power structures to addressing systemic issues that impact People of Color more often than Whites. At the same time, I was constantly encouraged by the honest engagement that my congregation exhibited to talk about racial and economic justice issues and realities in our community that few other churches seemed interested in addressing. But, even with this openness of mind, our congregation tended to attract mostly White progressives and only a few People of Color. Rather than confronting issues of race, we prided ourselves on being a welcoming congregation for gays and lesbians and for standing up against homophobia in our denomination. Consequently, racial issues were never as existential or urgent for our otherwise theologically and socially progressive congregation.

After the death of my wife in 1998, I met Michelle, a Presbyterian volunteer in mission from Michigan who came to Austin to work for three months in the Presbyterian ministry focused on helping people with health care and basic needs. We dated for several months and then began a long-distance relationship until we decided to get married at the beginning of 2000. Michelle was originally from Pittsburgh, so she had not experienced the kind of overt racism and the more subtle forms of racism that still existed in the South. Her interests in mission work in Mexico and Central America became a focus for our church and us during the first decade of the twenty-first century. After developing a mission project in Mexico and making many trips down there, our attention turned toward the racial and economic barriers that Latinos on both sides of the border were experiencing. I learned quickly that Latinos were also easy targets for those of us with White racial biases and economic fears and resentments. After receiving a sabbatical grant, Michelle and I went to Mexico and Costa Rica to learn Spanish so we could work more effectively to address the economic and racial difficulties that Latinos were facing.

A few years before I retired from active ministry, the Presbyterian racial strategy in Austin was to develop a congregation that appeals to racial minorities and to Whites seeking to address racial inequalities. A church in the city that had nearly died out called a young African American pastor who would appeal to those who were committed to a racially mixed ministry. This effort allowed the rest of our White churches to avoid the complexity and difficulties of addressing racial issues that were not existential for our congregations. As I retired, I lamented that, with some isolated exceptions, Sunday mornings continue to be some of the most racially segregated times in American society, and I had done little to address this racial divide in my own progressive congregation. Sadly, this racial reality doesn't seem to trouble most churches, whether they are White, Black, or Brown.

After retiring in 2012, I became involved in a local racial reconciliation effort in Georgetown, Texas, where I now live. Shortly after moving here, a mixed-race group of faith leaders in our community came together after the shooting of Michael Brown, Jr. in Ferguson, Missouri, to discuss how racial issues are manifested in our community. For over a year, we engaged in open, honest, and respectful conversations for three hours once a month about our personal experiences with racism and racial justice issues. Out of that sharing, we developed Courageous Conversations Georgetown, a faith-based initiative to "promote a culture of justice and compassion in Georgetown for people of all races and economic, religious, and ethnic identities." This community organization has engaged our community in racial justice and equity forums and has developed initiatives around public safety, affordable housing, public education, economic improvement, access to health care, and equity training, especially as these relate the racial issues.

One of the benefits of these conversations about racial issues with People of Color has been the broadening of my White racial framing about racial injustices that continue to take place in America. This experience has taught me the importance of hearing the stories and experiences of People of Color living in a predominantly White society. After participating in these local racial reconciliation conversations for a year or so, my wife suggested we attend one of the predominately African American churches in town as a deliberate effort to build some friendships with more People of Color. Michelle noted that bridging the racial divide in our community would be difficult for us simply because we live in our vastly White retirement community. So, we started visiting a small African American congregation near downtown, not knowing what to expect. Even though we were the only White people attending the worship service, we were warmly welcomed by the pastor and the members of that church. After a couple of Sundays worshiping with this congregation, it dawned on me that this was the first time in my life that I was the racial minority. This self-awareness in itself began to alter my perceptions about my racial identity and my own racial biases.

In the beginning, our Courageous Conversations group was a small cadre of Whites from seven or eight congregations in Georgetown working together with a small number of African Americans and Latinos from a handful of Black churches and the local Roman Catholic Church. We made the effort to reach out to more than fifty churches in our town, but few demonstrated much interest in addressing racial reconciliation in our community. It seemed to me that most White churches only think about praying for healing or forgiveness when a racially charged tragedy occurs. My own Presbyterian denomination acknowledged more than twenty years ago that troubling patterns of racial segregation and discrimination continue to take place in American life. However, after studying these racial issues, my denomination noted that "Christians are passive in the face of attacks on affirmative action and the adoption of regressive social policies at the local, state, and national levels." In a moment of rare honesty, the Presbyterian Church (USA) confessed that we needed "a new understanding of racism that takes into consideration the centrality of power in the institutionalization and perpetuation of racism."[1]

Despite all the good analysis of the dynamics of racism that my denomination conducted out of its stated desire to build what Martin Luther King, Jr. described as the Beloved Community, little effort or progress appeared to have been made within most White congregations to move toward that dream. I concluded that most White churches and their leaders are like many of our civic leaders—quick to condemn racial violence, hatred, and discrimination but are slow to mount any active or sustained efforts to address the causes or underlying issues that give rise to these tragedies.

I hope this personal narrative of my journey struggling with the dynamics of White racism will help readers understand why I call myself a "recovering racist." In my more idealized moments, I like to think of myself as an "anti-racist." But the truth is, I have been shaped throughout my entire life by a particular White racial identity with numerous White racial biases. I know better today than to judge people simply by the differences in the complexions of our skin. However, I still struggle at times to get beyond my White racial identity when I encounter People of Color. I know full well that old racial biases which divide humanity into "races" are a ludicrous and irrational way to make judgments about people. From all my experiences dealing with race issues, I have concluded that race relations in America have always been a complex and troubling issue, especially for those of us who have been deeply and subtly infected by old White biases rooted in a combination of assumed racial superiority, fear, and maintaining power over "others" not like us. Yet, I want to acknowledge that, for all the progress I have made, I still have to work at overcoming some of the residual and deeply embedded elements of my inherited White racism. Having BIPOC friends who will point out my racial blind spots is an important element in my ongoing recovery process.

I suspect that this confession will lead some people to conclude that my struggle with racism is more generational and more cultural than what other Whites have experienced. This is certainly a valid point of view. At times my racial biases have felt like preconscious, learned attitudes and behaviors instilled in me in my childhood, much like my being left-handed. The southern culture I grew up in certainly shaped and reinforced the racism I inherited from my family of origin.

Thankfully, many White people like my wife have not been as culturally indoctrinated with racism as I was growing up in the Deep South during the 1950-60s. When I have shared my personal history with racism with other White people, some have been shocked by the blatantly racist attitudes that I experienced in my early life simply because they were not exposed to such overt forms of racism. Consequently, many Whites do not need to overcome the degree of racial biases that my confession reveals. But some of those with whom I have shared my history of recovery from racism have confirmed that they too struggle with similar histories and issues with racial biases. When we discuss troubling racial issues in America today with one another, I have found that it can be liberating for Whites to express our own embarrassing stories, struggles, and experiences with racism. The sharing of these stories with one another, as difficult and self-critical as they often are, actually confirms for us what we would otherwise like to hide or forget, namely, that many of us who are White have been deeply infected by some measure of racial biases.

As I was working on this book, an older White friend of mine told me about his experience serving as a minister of music in a large White church in Alabama during the late 1960s. He recalled with sadness the night he was leading a church choir rehearsal when the news came in that MLK had been assassinated in Memphis. He can still feel the shock and disgust that came over him when some of his church choir members broke out in applause that night when they heard the news of King's assassination. It may be difficult for many of us today to think that such repugnant White racist ideas still exist among us. However, as frequent racial tragedies continue to take place around our nation, we may need to wake up and recognize we still have work to do to overcome the racism that persists with those of us who are White.

Nonetheless, my own recovery process has led me to be hopeful about the prospects of White people dealing with our deeply embedded racial biases at whatever levels these biases may reside within us. At this point in our nation's history, many of us are just now coming to appreciate how the legacy of racial genocide, slavery, Jim Crow laws, segregation, and institutional racism continue to impact race relations in this country. Some of us White-skinned people are learning, however reluctantly or slowly it might be, about the subtleties of racism and the discrimination that People of Color continue to experience on a regular basis. Only in the last few years have some of us found the strength and courage to recognize how our White skin tone grants us certain privileges and opportunities that People of Color do not enjoy. In some respects, these gradual racial understandings have not moved us very far as a nation in purging ourselves of evils of white superiority.

Yes, I gladly acknowledge that many of us who are White have made some significant progress during my lifetime dealing with both our racial biases and the evils of racism. My generation has lived through what has been called the "racial revolution in America" that emerged out of the civil rights movement of the 1950s and 1960s. This racial awakening in America was reinforced by the assassinations of MLK and Malcolm X, the Black power demonstrations by African American athletes at the 1968 Olympic Games, movies like *Guess Who's Coming to Dinner* and later TV shows like *All in the Family*, the passage of civil rights legislation in 1964, and in our appreciation for books like Alex Haley's *Roots*, Harper Lee's *To Kill a Mockingbird*, and Alice Walker's *The Color Purple*.

Certainly, the integration of public schools and the passing of equal rights legislation have helped us move beyond the defining skin color lines of the past. As more People of Color have moved into the mainstream of American culture, we have also seen an appreciation for the contributions that non-Whites have made to the character of our nation. However, as I said earlier, any optimism we may have about the end of racism in America should now be shattered by the unrelenting landslide of news reports over the past decade alone about discriminatory racial practices and White violence against People of Color. For those of us willing to notice, the social inequities created from the White institutional racism of the past are still evident. African Americans and Latinx have also exerted their own racial identities and place in American society in ways that many of us now celebrate. In recent years, we have seen the building of museums to tell the honest history of racial discrimination while claiming and celebrating the cultural contributions that People of Color have made in education, music, sports, and the arts, as well as attaining important political leadership roles. In some ways, we may have recently turned a new chapter in the racial revolution of America with enlarged White racial awareness and attitudes, including the willingness among many of us to honestly face our nation's tragic history of racism. We will now see what impact this new racial awareness may have.

By sharing this personal developmental history, my hope is that White readers will be encouraged to engage in their own self-examination of how they may have bought into White racial constructs about White superiority, White privilege, and institutional biases that harm People of Color. As my confession suggests, I believe our redemptive journey in dismantling racism begins with our willingness to recognize and acknowledge how our racial biases have shaped both our individual lives and the institutional structures under which we live. In doing this kind of self-examination and historical reckoning, we are also accepting a share of the responsibility for bringing an end to the White racial preferences that undermine America's culture of diversity and our highest moral and social values.

Looking back on it, my own recovery from the racial indoctrination I received in my childhood was predicated on three critical factors: 1) The contradictions I noticed between the professed religious ideals and moral values of the adults in my life and their behavior towards People of Color; 2) My first-hand conversations and experiences with People of Color; and 3) A willingness to be introspective about my racial identity and to have empathy toward those with other identities. I am well aware that some Whites in this country do not share some or any of these dispositions and attitudes. So, reflective changes in attitudes about racial issues may not be possible for those who are locked into defending White racial identities and moral goodness.

When discussing with other Whites the challenges involved in addressing our racial biases, I am often asked if I am hopeful about the prospects of America ever overcoming our legacy with racism. Yes, I am. Thankfully, younger generations of White-skinned people have had less exposure to the racial biases of the past and have developed an appreciation for people whose skin color may be different than their own. I have celebrated this reality within my own family. While writing this book, I received a picture of our oldest granddaughter all dressed up for her high school prom. To my delight, her date for the prom was an African American young man in her school that she likes. So, the times they are changing.

CHAPTER TWO
RECOGNIZING THE PERVASIVENESS OF OUR RACIAL BIASES

"A fantastic system of evasions, denials, and justifications, which system is about to destroy [white men's] grasp of reality, which is another way of saying their moral sense."

—James Baldwin

As I hope my confession reveals, I never considered myself to be an avowed White supremacist, nor have I ever endorsed racism in any form at any time during my life. But I trust my confession makes it clear that I have had to struggle to free myself from the racial biases I learned in my formative years growing up in the Deep South. Recognizing this racist heritage is not a personal admission that I make with either shame or guilt. This is simply an honest acknowledgment of my acquired racial biases that I have had to confront and overcome during my lifetime.

Like most White people, I didn't choose to be a racist or consciously adopt racist beliefs. In many respects, I became an "accidental" racist simply because I absorbed the White southern cultural norms of the 1950s and 1960s that shaped my racial self-identification and the relationships in my childhood. As sad as it is to say today, there was no moral or religious judgment against being a White racist in the culture of my youth. My social environment maintained in both overt and subtle ways the belief that White-skinned people were just inherently better in numerous ways—intellectually, culturally, ethically—than people with dark skin colors. In my teen and early adult years, I heard and learned all the explanations and justifications that White people often gave to support this viewpoint about White superiority and "Negro" inferiority. Even as I was working my way out from under these White racial biases, I moved to Texas and discovered that Mexican Americans had been targeted for generations by the same type of White racial biases that were aimed at African Americans in Florida, where I was raised.

From my perspective today, such beliefs seem tragically misguided and the source of massive amounts of evil that have been inflicted for generations on people with darker skin colors by people with light skin color. I learned in college that this racist attitude about skin colors has been pervasive in American history and perpetuated mainly by Whites for generations. Up until the 1960s, White racism was legally and socially reinforced in particular regions of this country by segregated "White and Colored" restrooms and water fountains, "separate but equal" public schools, Lilly White churches, and a host of social norms proclaiming White superiority concerning African Americans in particular. The use of racial slurs and epithets to refer to Black people was commonplace among Whites for the first twenty years of my life. It was not until I reached adulthood that I came to understand just how insidious and misguided my inherited racist views were.

In listening to the stories of People of Color, I have learned that more subtle forms of White racism still exist in America that most of us do not recognize. So, I have written this book from the perspective that it takes deliberate and sustained efforts on the part of White people for us to completely escape the tentacles of this socially constructed and communicated disease we refer to as racism. Calling myself "a recovering racist" is my attempt to demonstrate that I understand the myriad ways that Whites have inherited racial biases not of our own making. This is also my way of saying I know I have to constantly be aware of and work against the racial prejudices and White privileges that undermine the ideals of racial equality and justice I claim to affirm. Recovery, in this context, means I place myself among those who recognize we have some lingering racial biases from which we are struggling to free ourselves.

Like other Whites of my generation, I can look back now with embarrassment and even disbelief about these indoctrinated racial biases. In numerous conversations with other White-skinned people, I have also learned that what we might call "culturally-induced White racism" permeated not only our individual thinking and behavior but also shaped many of the dominant White social, political, economic, and religious institutional practices that have shaped this nation. The movie *The Green Book* illustrates both the personal and the cultural manifestations of the kind of White racism that inhabited large regions of America until the 1970s without much questioning.

Thankfully, many of us today have recanted the racial indoctrination we may have received from the past. In what amounts to a stunning transformation within a generation or two, most White people today claim to know better than to ever judge someone simply by the color of their skin. Nonetheless, I continue to hear older White people tell embarrassing stories to one another about how racism influenced our impressions and attitudes about noticeable racial differences among the people we have encountered in our lives. A retired friend my age, for instance, recalled traveling as a child on a train with his mother, going from their small town in Wisconsin to Milwaukee. While on the train, he noticed, for the first time in his life, a Black person. He innocently pointed to the Black woman and blurted out aloud, "Look, Mama, that lady has covered herself with Black shoe polish!" For a long time, he said, he did not understand why his mother was so embarrassed by his vocal observation about someone with a dark skin color that he had never seen before.

However innocent or subtle our racial categorizations may be, the fact is "White" has been both the dominant skin color in America and the most socially acceptable skin color a person can have. Nevertheless, one of the psychological wonders about some Whites in America today is our amnesia about how profoundly skin color by itself marked a badge of worth and respect for White-skinned people while devaluing people with dark skin tones.

One of the racism inflection points I see today is the willingness of Whites to honestly acknowledge that we have assimilated, unwittingly at times, some measure of a racial bias with a strong preference for being "White." For all the advances against racial discrimination we may have made over the past thirty years or more in America, I believe it is naive and dishonest for Whites to suggest that we have purged twenty generations of racism from our collective consciousness just within the last one or two generations.

Racial research studies of kindergarten teachers in recent years have revealed, for instance, the presence of implicit White biases among teachers who interact with mixed racial students in their classrooms. There continue to be far too many incidences of racial discrimination going on in this country today for us to pretend that racism and White racial biases are a thing of the past. Before any of us should be so bold as to suggest that we have overcome America's racist past, we need to ask any person of color about their experiences with White people and our White-controlled institutions. My conversations with People of Color have led me to realize that we still have a lot of work to do to overcome long-standing racial biases. Among the racial biases I am working on at this point in my life is my belief that most White people have been infected to some degree by racial biases that we often do not recognize or acknowledge to ourselves or anyone else. The racial bias recovery process outlined in this book starts with being clear about what constitutes "racism" and embedded White racial biases.

Getting Beyond Difficulties with Definitions

When I attempt to talk about racial biases with White people today, I often encounter questions about the meaning of terms like "racism" and "White privilege." Many Whites become very defensive about any suggestion that we may hold "racist" attitudes or beliefs. So, it is important for us to define and unpack what we mean by the word "racism" in order to address the contentiousness this emotionally loaded and pejorative term generates for most White people.

Part of this difficulty revolves around our tendency to think of racism and racists in binary terms as an "either/or" condition or attitude that implies we are a bigoted person with a maladjusted belief system, or we are not. Consequently, most of us tend to think that only those White people who make bigoted claims about the superiority of White people or act in discriminatory ways toward People of Color deserve to be labeled as "racists." Many of us, therefore, confine "racists" to the emotionally misguided and hate-filled Whites like Dylann Roof, who went into an African American church in Charleston and murdered the pastor and seven others during a Bible study, or like Alex Fields, Jr., the twenty-one-year-old Hitler admirer who drove his car into a group of protesters in Charlottesville, Virginia, killing a young woman. Most of us are quick to reject the kind of racist phobia and rhetoric that gets spewed by White nationalists. The vast majority of Whites in America today recoil from any suggestion that "we," the decent and more enlightened Whites, may harbor racist beliefs or make judgments about people solely based on skin color. In short, we think of "racism" as a kind of ignorant and narrow-minded thinking reflected in bigots and self-avowed White supremacists.

To get beyond these reactive and defensive notions about racists and racism, it is important to carefully define these terms. Some of us think of racism in terms of prejudices, which all of us have about people, places, ideas, and most anything else we may have a strong preference for or dislike toward. As I noted in my introduction, "racism" is more accurately defined as a "system of advantages granted to some and not to others on the basis of race" (Wellman). As this definition implies, simply having a racial preference does not necessarily give someone an advantage over others, nor does a prejudice in itself allow one racial group of people to oppress another group. Many of us have racial biases, cultural preferences, and prejudices. Simply having a racial bias or preference does not necessarily make someone a racist.

As Beverly Daniel Tatum points out, racism occurs when the racial preferences that people with social power have allowed them to create or impose policies and practices that give them advantages while denying rights or privileges to others. Tatum argues as a Person of Color that any racial group can maintain hateful attitudes and behavior toward other racial groups. But, "racism" takes place when a particular racial group has the social, political, economic, and cultural power to impose its prejudices on other racial groups.[1] In terms of racism in America, the underlying prejudice that animated the genocide of the indigenous people on this continent, the enslavement of Africans, the injustices inflicted on Latinos and Asians, Jim Crow laws, racial segregation, and a host of other discriminatory practices was the belief in the inherent superiority of White people and the inferiority of People of Color.

Similarly, Jews in Europe during the advent of World War II became the targets of Nazi racism because of their German "master race" beliefs and their efforts to eradicate those they considered to be sub-human moral degenerates. **The key point here is that White racism in America reflects the *racial prejudices and power* that our dominant group has used to give those of us who are identified as "White" a constellation of social, economic, and political advantages while disadvantaging non-Whites who have been considered to be inferior or less capable.**

Some White people today like to claim they are "color-blind," presumably to distance themselves from the overt racist attitudes of past generations. To help Whites to move beyond thinking of racism and racists in negative binary terms, a noted sociologist who has studied racism suggests we should examine racial issues in terms of what he calls "the White racial frame." According to this conceptualization of race, the *White racial frame* conveys the idea of a shared socially and culturally constructed perspective about White identity issues that are deeply embedded in individual minds, as well as in collective memories and histories, to help people make sense out of every day relationships and situations.[2]

Psychologists and sociologists sometimes refer to what they call "implicit biases" to describe the preferences that White people often hold in terms of racial identities. Researchers have found that we all function in life in varying degrees with some "implicit racial biases" that have been shaped by direct and indirect negative information we received in childhood and that has been socially reinforced over time. Much of this research has focused on the unconscious prejudices and stereotypes that impact how we relate to others and see ourselves. Both of these conceptual viewpoints seek to help White people become more aware of the complex mental and social dynamics of racial discrimination while reducing our emotional defensiveness about having our presumed White virtues being attacked. I believe the challenge most of us face today is to become more aware of how we tend to frame racial issues and hold on to unconscious, implicit biases.

Racism Goes Way Beyond A "Few Bad Apple" Racists

One of the primary difficulties Whites have when we are asked to discuss our racial biases centers on our innate need to protect our own identity as being a "good" person. Not only are the terms "racism" and "racist" heavily loaded words with negative (and accusatory) connotations, but the way these terms are used often reveals the complexity of many different meanings. As anti-racism trainers point out, White people tend to think of racism in individual terms, as racial prejudices that individual people hold, whereas Black and Brown people generally think of racism in collective terms, as systems of power that White people have to control and negatively impact the lives of non-Whites. For some people, "racism" is seen as a prejudice about not liking someone based on skin color. In this sense, some of us claim that People of Color can also be racists. Others only think of "racism" in terms of individuals who mistreat or oppress someone because of their race and deny them their rights based on their skin color. When we are confronted with stories of White people acting in blatantly racist ways toward People of Color, it is not uncommon for us to think that these are just the bad apples among us.

None of these ideas reflect what I understand "racism" to be. A more sophisticated understanding of "racism" looks beyond individual attitudes to issues of power and oppression that a dominant group can use to impose their desires on a minority. From this perspective, "racism" entails a collective and institutional prejudice against a minority group (usually People of Color) by a dominant group (usually White) that leads to unfair treatments and injustices. The long-standing racial categorizing of people in our country is what Rev. Martin Luther King, Jr. was pointing to in his 1968 speech "The Other America," which he gave at Grosse Point High School in Michigan. He attempted to be honest about both the basis for this racism and the results of this racial segregation:

> *The first thing I would like to mention is that there must be a recognition on the part of everybody in this nation that America is still a racist country. Now however unpleasant that sounds, it is the truth. And we will never solve the problem of racism until there is a recognition of the fact that racism still stands at the center of so much of our nation and we must see racism for what it is. It is the nymph of an inferior people. It is the notion that one group has all of the knowledge, all of the insights, all of the purity, all of the work, all of the dignity. And another group is worthless, on a lower level of humanity, inferior. To put it in*

philosophical language, racism is not based on some empirical generalization which, after some studies, would conclude that these people are behind because of environmental conditions. Racism is based on an ontological affirmation. It is the notion that the very being of a people is inferior.

Because "racism" encompasses so many different dimensions of attitudes and behaviors, some of us want to argue that everyone is racist to the extent that we all prefer to associate socially and culturally with others who are like us; noting a naturally social and cultural tendency for "birds of a feather sticking together." Another version of this attempt to sidestep the importance of racial identities in America is to reduce "racism" to the stereotyping of people who are different from us in some noticeable ways (do not share our native language, culture, history, as well as skin coloration). There is no doubt that the human tendency toward "othering the stranger" takes place in many cultures besides our own (e.g., ethnic Koreans are discriminated against in Japan, Jews have been discriminated against in many Christian countries, etc.). Some Whites in America even complain about "reverse discrimination" when Affirmative Action laws provide People of Color with certain opportunities that may have been historically denied because they were not seen as being White. Such arguments about the need to remove any unfairness between the races today fail to recognize the impact of the dehumanizing history and disadvantages that People of Color have suffered in this country for generations at the hands of the White majority who had the power to oppress them.

Lastly, it is important to recognize that "racism" is not confined to just one or two expressions of discrimination based on noticeable differences in skin color. While all of us may have some particular prejudices about people who are not like us, this does not in itself lead to thinking or treating them as unequal or inferior to us. Nor should we lump all White people together as sharing a certain type of racial bias or behaving out of the same discriminatory attitude.

Instead of using the inflammatory term "racism" to talk about White identity issues, I try to use a less reactive way of referring to our White racial "problem." So, I often will use the terms "White racial biases" to refer to *our* notions about race. By "White racial bias," I simply mean any shared set of inherited beliefs that consider White-skinned people to be more virtuous and inherently superior to people with darker skin colors in some undefined way that is neither biologically nor socially justifiable.

It has become clear to me from reading the study conducted by Dorothy Roberts in her book *Fatal Invention: How Science, Politics, and Big Business Re-Create Race in the Twenty-first Century* that the idea of "race" is itself a manufactured term created centuries ago by White Europeans as a social demarcation implying sub-species within the one human family. Roberts investigates the genetic and biological research that reveals "human beings do not fit the zoological definition of race" and dividing people into these categories is a "political practice" rather than a scientific one. While she notes there are scientific studies about the genetic links in ancestry and environment within the human family, Roberts points to the fact that changing beliefs about what constitutes racial differences between Whites and Blacks in the course of American history in itself undermines the idea of some natural division in races that is easily recognized. When we begin to see how the concept of "race" is a social invention rather than a biological classification, it becomes apparent that racial identity matters most to those who wish to claim some uniqueness or advantages for themselves. Nevertheless, in recognizing that race is a political system, Roberts suggests that we cannot ditch the idea of race altogether but must "use political means to end its harmful impact on our society."

What makes acknowledging White racial biases so difficult for many of us to own is our failure to recognize is the ubiquity of our racial identity in a predominately White society where skin color has granted us certain privileges and opportunities that People of Color have not been given. Racism took hold in America primarily because White people who controlled the institutions of power in this nation could dictate legal, economic, political, social, and moral privileges for some and deny these to others based on skin color, along with biases about gender and cultural norms as well. U.S. history from the Civil War to the Civil Rights Act of 1964 can easily be read as the national struggle of White people to address some of the seventeenth and eighteenth-century European ideas about the racial superiority of White-skinned people over darker-skinned people.

Our nation's struggles with racism during the civil rights era made us acutely aware of the contradictions in our purported values of social equality and freedom. Since the 1970s, our whole country has been subjected to moments of self-examination about our racist history and our White racial biases through poignant television shows, literature, movies, music, and other art forms that have attempted to tell the uncomfortable truth about the racial character of America to this day. I believe this recognition of our cultural heritage of White racial biases is critically important and slow in coming but needs to be amplified in order to eradicate racism in this country.

Let me quickly add that we have made significant, and at times painful, progress over the past fifty years in overcoming many of the ugliest and evil forms of overt White racism that killed, damaged, or ruined the lives of so many People of Color in this nation. Yet, we should not be lulled into believing that our racial biases no longer exist or no longer negatively impact non-White people today. The past decade alone has demonstrated that White fear, White resentments, White dominance, and White control continue to inflict harm, hurt, and death on People of Color. The litany of names in the news in recent years—Michael Brown, Jr., Travon Martin, Freddie Gray, Breonna Taylor, Ahmaud Arbery, George Floyd—should make it clear to all of us that White racial biases still impact non-Whites in horrific ways. Likewise, the disproportionate incarceration rates among People of Color in our criminal justice system and the economic and wealth disparities between Whites and People of Color ought to demonstrate the same realities.

Even more telling perhaps are the White defensive arguments that arise when tragic racial "incidents" occur or racial disparities are pointed out—the easy judgments that these racial minorities had only suffered the consequences of not respecting law enforcement officers or they were engaged in some criminal activity. When someone notes that America is still a heavily racially divided and socially segregated country, the new White explanation is that this reality simply reflects the tendency among racial groups to interact with those most like us, suggesting that social relationships are formed more by shared cultural values and economic class than by racial identities. Some even argue that economic and cultural differences contribute to our social biases more than racial differences. To me, all of these arguments sound like a desire to maintain racial innocence by blaming the victims of violence and racial discrimination rather than acknowledging that our racial biases do negatively shape race relations in our country in a host of ways we do not like to acknowledge. As long as Whites continue to deny any responsibility for the racial inequities or injustices that show up today, I believe that many People of Color will never escape the perils of being seen and treated as second-class citizens in America.

The development of my own racial self-awareness over the years has led me to recognize that many of my White biases are deeply embedded in me in ways that I do not like to admit. So, my way of looking at my own implicit racial biases is to think of myself as someone recovering from an emotional and social disease much in the same way we think about those recovering from a mental illness or from substance addiction. My interactions with both Whites and People of Color have impressed upon me the realization that many of us continue to be infected to some degree by the subtle racial biases that have been transmitted to us socially and culturally from previous generations. But I want to be quick to say that the degree to which each of us may have inherited some measure of racial bias varies greatly among those of us who are White. Moreover, I don't think it is constructive for us to divide Whites into binary groups so as to think some of us are "racists" while others of us are "anti-racists," implying that this distinction can be determined by some attitudinal litmus test or dividing line.

As my own confession has demonstrated, attitudinal change often takes place over time when we have new life experiences that do not square with our previously held beliefs. During my lifetime, I have witnessed an extraordinary evolution in the views and attitudes about race and race relations among White people in this country, mainly because of the social interactions that challenged old racial stereotypes. Yes, we still have self-proclaiming White supremacists among us, but we also have conscious anti-racists among us as well. When it comes to racial biases, most of us fall somewhere along a continuum from having many White racial biases to having few to none.

One of my African American friends has suggested from his experience working as the city manager in a large U.S. city that White people often individually reflect one of four stages of White racial biases: 1) overt/self-proclaiming racists, 2) indifferent/unconscious racists, 3) ambivalent/apologetic racists, and 4) self-aware/anti-racists. The point being racial biases show up to greater or lesser degrees in most of us who are White. So, rather than engaging in denial or protecting our own racial identity, it is more helpful for all of us to ask ourselves where we fall along a broad continuum of White racial biases. This might help us avoid the presumption that we are free from generations of racial bias and move beyond defending ourselves as virtuous White people who are not implicated in any way in the institutional forms of racism that still exist in America to this day.

As I have stated, my intention in writing this book is not to promote White guilt, shame, or blame for the racial sins of the past, either individually or collectively. Getting stuck in these emotional reactions to the history of racism will not help us to dismantle the vestiges of our racial biases. If achieving greater racial equity is a defining challenge in America today, then our goal should be to uphold the belief in the dignity and worth of every person and to promote equal opportunities for all in the pursuit of the common good. To suggest that all White people continue to be trapped in stereotypes about skin color or ethnic ancestry is no more helpful than to suggest that non-Whites depend on the conversion of all White people into anti-racists in order to achieve freedom, equality, or success. As John McWhorter, an African American professor of English at Columbia University, has noted, "In my life, racism has affected me now and then at the margins, in very occasional social ways, but has had no effect on my access to societal resources; if anything, it has made them more available to me than they would have been otherwise. Nor should anyone dismiss me as a rara avis. Being middle class, upwardly mobile, and Black has been quite common during my existence since the mid-1960s, and to deny this is to assert that affirmative action for Black people did not work."[3]

McWhorter is just one of many People of Color in this country today who have not been crippled by whatever levels of White racial biases they may have faced in their lives. To dismiss these People of Color as "exceptional" or to claim they are proof that racial biases no longer handicap anyone overlooks the challenges present today in the glaring inequities that still exist between Whites and non-Whites in America.

At the same time, McWhorter cautions against using the term "White supremacist" to brand anyone who may challenge the particular values or attitudes of a Person of Color. He argues for making a careful distinction between a White person who has a racial bias and a "White supremacist." To his way of thinking, White racial biases are not tantamount to notions about White superiority. He says, "The fact that psychological tests reveal subtle racial biases in Whites does not justify calling any White person's questioning of the views of a Person of Color a White supremacist. That's an athletic jump from the subtle to the stark, from the subliminal to the egregious."[4]

I find it difficult, nevertheless, to determine how a White person's racial bias does not include some hint of White superiority. Maybe some White people can make a racially neutral observation about someone's darker skin color without implying a sense of White superiority. What I don't understand is how we might have a "racial bias" without some presumption about racial preference or judgment. Perhaps McWhorter is simply trying not to impugn all White people as being "racists" by reserving the term "White supremacist" for those of us who intentionally make negative value judgments about People of Color because their skin is not White.

Recognizing the Diversions and Justifications We Make

It is also important to note here that some Whites attempt to side-step the issue of racial biases and racism by arguing that individual responsibility is more critical than race in promoting and achieving social equity for African Americans and other People of Color. This diversion away from White racial biases is often expressed by White ideological conservatives who argue that the lack of individual initiative and/or poor morality explains why many African Americans or Latinos suffer disproportionately from poverty or have bad experiences with law enforcement and the criminal justice system, or have problems with substance abuse.

Many of those who take this position also claim that African Americans are prone to playing "the race card" to avoid accepting responsibility for their own cultural, social, and economic failures. Some even go so far as to say that the Black Lives Matter movement is dangerous because it undermines civic respect for law enforcement and the importance of obeying the law. Rather than recognizing the residual legacy of poverty and second-class citizenship that White racial biases have created for African Americans and Latinos, these conservative voices like to point out that minorities must confront their own dysfunctional behavior and attitudes in order to achieve higher levels of social, economic, and legal equity in this country. The assumption is that White racial biases today have a relatively minor negative impact on African Americans or Latinos, unlike in the past. Those Whites who hold this viewpoint like to claim that everyone in America, regardless of racial identities, stands now on a level playing field, and it is primarily up to racial minorities to earn their social acceptance, educational opportunities, civil rights, and economic success within today's color-blind democracy.

As Imani Perry has carefully noted, racial identities today are not simply based on distinctive human skin colors but often include stereotypes based on cultural differences in the use of language, preferences in music, dress, style, and other shared associations with particular racial groups. This suggests that today's racial biases are not the same as yesterday's in that some of the old White biases are often masked by politeness, tolerance, and political correctness. Many Whites today share the outrage of People of Color when overt racist behavior or racial injustices occur. Rather than getting bogged down in debates about the amount of racial progress we may have made in America, Perry would have us ask this question: How is our nation continuing to create people who act in ways that sustain the racial inequality that is very evident in America today?[5] She recognizes that People of Color can exhibit negative stereotypes and cultural criticism of their own racial group that ends up promoting racial inequality. I believe that White people also have to ask the additional question: Why do we act in ways that sustain racial inequalities in America when we claim our nation upholds the principles of equality, democracy, and justice for all?

I certainly agree that we should not lower expectations for anyone simply because of the color of their skin. To do so socially, educationally, or politically robs people of their dignity and keeps them from achieving their potential. No doubt some Whites, and maybe some government programs, have related to People of Color out of a sense of guilt because of our nation's racist history. Yes, we might find some examples of how government welfare programs aimed at helping People of Color have sometimes created, inadvertently, generational dependencies on welfare assistance and/or impeded individual responsibility for bettering one's life. But I think it is both naive and idealistic to assume that the civil rights movement or Equal Opportunity legislation have now created a level playing field for Whites and People of Color. So, when I hear conservative White people and successful People of Color blame the victims of generational racism for their conditions, I suspect that some form of White denial or racial indifference resides in their attitudes. Given that many White people find refuge in these beliefs that personal responsibility is the culprit that handicaps People of Color more than racism, I want to address this perspective in some detail.

Thomas Sowell, an African American intellectual, is perhaps the leading spokesperson over the past three decades for this conservative perspective that personal behavior is a more critical factor than racism for the social equity of People of Color. In Sowell's view, racism hasn't hindered African Americans from obtaining social or economic equity in America as much as the failure of African Americans to adopt mainstream, middle-class Anglo-American values and behaviors in order to enjoy the benefits of our progressive society. He argues that many African Americans, particularly in the South and even among those who immigrated to the North, have taken on the characteristics of the White "redneck" culture that became prevalent in the South with the influx of poorly educated Scottish immigrants into that region of the country in the nineteenth century. He claims this "Black sub-culture" has produced a set of dysfunctional values and destructive behaviors that prevent many African Americans from achieving more social equity—shunning education, engaging in sexual promiscuity, resorting to the use of violence to express frustrations, being averse to working, and searching for excitement rather than disciplined economic success. Sowell claims that White liberals have exacerbated these "Black redneck" attributes among African Americans by suggesting racism is the problem and creating dependency among African Americans on government welfare programs.[4]

Interestingly, Sowell also places some of the blame for this generational Black failure on African American church leaders who promote "a religious oratory" that presumably encourages "unbridled emotions" and the promise of next-world salvation rather than personal responsibility for today's living conditions. He claims that low educational expectations of African American children and mistaken classroom educational practices have also contributed to the problems we often attribute to race. About the only responsibility Sowell sees that White people have had in crippling African Americans can be traced back to the Emancipation Proclamation when enslaved Africans in America were not given the capacity—presumably with land, education, and opportunities—"to function as responsible members of a free society."[6]

Historically, he says, slavery has not been a peculiarly White crime nor a peculiarly American crime. In Sowell's proclaimed pragmatism, he seems to imply that White America has simply and erroneously allowed large segments of African Americans to become dependent, helpless individuals who are living in a "thug culture." This individualistic ideology ends up blaming any or all victims of racism for their own social, economic, and political deficits. Consequently, Sowell has become a poster child advocate for conservative Whites who prefer to indict People of Color for their collective failures to live up to their freedoms and responsibilities rather than acknowledge any role that White racial biases and privileges may have played in keeping African Americans marginalized.

Bill O'Reilly, the conservative White TV political commentator and bestselling author, suggests that racism is less a problem for African Americans today than the fragmentation of Black families has become. He claims the levels of violence and chaos that exist in many Black communities are due to the disintegration of African American families with higher percentages of children born out of wedlock and with absentee fathers. In his view, young Black men are involved in more crime and end up in the criminal justice system because of this family fragmentation problem within the African American community itself. It's O'Reilly's statement, "White people don't force Black people to have babies out of wedlock; that's their personal decision that leads to social and economic disaster," that sounds like White defensiveness, which ignores the effects of institutional racism.

While his thinking appeals to those who tout the importance of individual responsibility for achieving social and economic success, there's no recognition in this perspective that dominant White culture has created and perpetuated for generations social structures that have contributed to the fragmentation of African American families since the days of slavery. In O'Reilly's mind, White privilege and ideas about White superiority are things of the past. So, People of Color today should not be excused for their failures to achieve or prosper in this society. To me, this is a conveniently racist-tinged way of overlooking and minimizing the history of racial discrimination and injustices that have crippled African American citizens from the earliest days of this country. I hear attitudes like this as an effort to avoid White responsibility for racism by blaming the victims of racism for their failure to overcome the legacy of White biases that have shaped this country for generations. This line of thinking would have us believe that the civil rights movement and our own cultural appreciation for diversity have now created a level educational, economic, and social playing field for everyone regardless of our racial backgrounds. My experience and the experience of many others tell me this perspective is naive at best and racist at worst.

On the other end of the spectrum, there are White people who believe that the only way to overcome racism is for it to be bred out of us eventually via inter-racial marriages and the growth of multiracial offspring. Some like to think this pragmatic evolutionary idea about future generations of mixed-race humanity will move us beyond the skin color distinctions of the past. For them, history suggests that lighter-skinned African Americans have been assimilated into the dominant White culture in America with greater ease and acceptability than darker-skinned African Americans have. No doubt, the proliferation of mixed-race children in America will certainly challenge some of the old notions about White superiority, maintaining the purity of races, and categorizing people on the basis of their racial ancestry. However, this perspective simply kicks the can of White racism down the road to some future possibility in history rather than addressing the White bias problems of today. More than anything, this is another way some people prefer to minimize that legacy of White racial biases on People of Color in this country.

There is yet another philosophical perspective that provides blinders as to how hegemonic White racism has shaped America. Conservative columnist David Brooks suggests that the political, social, and economic virtues of America grew out of a spirit of individualism and personal liberty. He cites Jonah Goldberg's claim about the "miracle" of American prosperity and accomplishments by saying, "the miracle ushered in a philosophy that says each person is to be judged and respected on account of their own merits, not the class or caste of their ancestors."

Brooks says, "That belief, championed by John Locke, or a story we tell about Locke, paved the way for human equality, pluralism, democracy, capitalism and the idea that a person can have a plurality of identities and a society can contain a plurality of moral creeds. It also proved to be the goose that laid the golden egg. Economic growth exploded. The American founding asserted that Lockean ideas are universal. And nothing had ever succeeded like America. Between 1860 and 1900 alone, America's population doubled and its wealth grew fivefold."

While this spirit of individualism and effort may explain White prosperity, it completely ignores the plight of African Americans, not only during the last half of the nineteenth century but right up to today. No doubt this ideal about individualism may have contributed to White prosperity in America, but the ancestors of People of Color certainly did not escape the White imposed structures of class, caste, or race. Again, White people tend to read history and to espouse moral virtues on the basis of our White racial frame rather than from the vantage point of People of Color who have not benefited as much from the institutional structures our White descendants put in place.

It seems to me that for any more significant progress to be made in race relations in this country, both White people and People of Color must work together to dismantle the legacy of racism that shows up in today's racial disparities. To overlook White racial biases rooted in White superiority and White privileges, as subtle are these often are, is no more responsible than to claim People of Color are to blame for whatever problems they now face. Given the dominance of Whites in shaping social policies and institutions, I believe that we have the largest share of the responsibility for achieving the kind of racial reconciliation and equity we say we want and need. Much of the work I think needs to be done involves our willingness and ability to let go of the White racial frame that elevates "Whiteness" as a social and cultural ideal over other skin colors. Like James Baldwin, the African American writer, observed more than fifty years ago, "The American ideal of racial progress is measured by how fast I become White." To overcome this preference toward Whiteness, I believe we must find the courage, the emotional strength, and the social commitment to recognize the pervasiveness of White racial biases, and these biases continue to impact People of Color. To that end, Whites must stop looking for racial diversions and justifications that blame People of Color for racial inequalities.

This begs the question, of course, about Whites being charged with the responsibility to "bring an end to old ideas about the inherent superiority of Whiteness." Honestly, there is only so much that Persons of Color can do to help those of us who are White with our problem. Too many of us continue to assume that People of Color need to conform to the values, attitudes, and behaviors that the White community has established. This viewpoint also has racist underpinnings.

Drawing upon Toni Morrison's moral perspective on dealing with White racists, columnist Charles Blow has noted: "Racism is a moral corruption built on an intellectual fallacy and exists as a construction invented for the very purpose of violence. So, when people demonstrate that they subscribe to theories of racism, they have shown their hand, and I am immediately roused by the euphoric understanding that they are compromised, diminished and assailable."[7]

As Blow says, racist comments by White people don't hurt his feelings because he sees the moral imperfections in their attitudes. But he is enraged, rightfully so, "when racists are granted power in society to allow their idiocy to have a negative impact on other people, whether that be culturally, psychologically, and spiritually, or materially and physically."

So, the first step in the racism recovery process I am promoting begins with recognizing, rather than ignoring or evading, how White racial biases have shaped our individual lives, our nation's history, and our institutions with respect to People of Color. Once we can honestly acknowledge the pervasiveness of White racial biases among us, we will need to address the emotional uncomfortableness that many Whites feel when we are asked to discuss racial issues. I suspect that many of us know intuitively that we are implicated in some way or form in this White social disease.

CHAPTER THREE
MOVING BEYOND DENIAL

"Only the racist lives by the heartbeat of denial. The anti-racist lives by the opposite heartbeat, one that rarely and irregularly sounds in America—the heartbeat of confession."

—Ibram X. Kendi

It's fairly easy for most of us who are White to forget how deeply entrenched racism has been in the history of America. Thankfully, we have made significant progress over the past five decades in addressing some of the worst forms of racial bias that were legally and politically institutionalized in various ways throughout this country. The "White" and "Colored" signs for restrooms and the segregated public schools that lasted in the South until the 1970s are gone. Interracial marriages are no longer a White social taboo reinforced by state laws. It has now been over fifty years since the civil rights movement successfully confronted White America with the massive contradictions between our ideals of equality and justice for all and the way People of Color have been treated in our nation's history. Many of us today like to think that the oppressive reach of racial biases is largely a thing of the past.

With the end of these obviously racist practices in the past, most of us want to believe we have purged ourselves of the ideology of

White superiority, and we no longer judge people by their skin color. We know that White supremacists and White Nationalists who spew vitriol about People of Color still exist. We are aware that some of us also express animosity toward Jews, Muslims, LGBTQ people, immigrants, and others who may be seen as a threat to our national identity and values. Nonetheless, many of us now claim to be socially enlightened, and we try to minimize the presence of the overt racists and suggest they are not representative of most of us. Yes, we know a few fearful Whites sometimes resort to violence to express their biases against otherwise innocent people that they have come to detest. But we distance ourselves both psychologically and morally from them.

When a gunman enters a synagogue in Pittsburgh and murders worshiping congregants, or when a crazed young man hunts down and kills Latinos in a Walmart store in El Paso, many of us are quick to label such people as being mentally ill rather than racists. When White supremacists and Neo-Nazis show up in public today defending Confederate monuments or demanding the right to speak on college campuses, we prefer to claim they are the uneducated White anomaly who are not reflective of the progress the rest of us have made in our racial attitudes. With these disclaimers, we create a dualistic viewpoint about White racial attitudes and behaviors in this country. In essence, we tell ourselves and People of Color and religious minorities that it is important to somehow sort out the "good" White people from the "bad" White people. This mindset allows us to avoid addressing the deeper-seated White beliefs and biases that continue to motivate racist violence and perpetuate racial injustices.

My experience addressing race issues in the last decade has led me to believe that most White people in America today are living in some state of denial or gross naivete about the lingering aspects of White racial biases in this country. Let me offer here only three examples of how this pervasive denial and blindness about racial biases show up among us today.

First, many of us think we can accurately determine the existence of our racial biases within or among us without relying on what People of Color who experience White biases may suggest is the case. This sense of self-determined objectivity about the presence of racial discrimination is both arrogant and unfounded. It also serves as a convenient way for us to avoid or deny the presence of White racial bias that we may unconsciously harbor. Women who have experienced gender bias issues in the workplace know very well that men often do not recognize the various ways that our male biases show up in our working relationships and expectations. Without welcoming feedback from People of Color about our implicit or unconscious racial biases, we often live with the fantasy that we are color-blind and free from any form of White racism. Our denial about our racial biases has become widespread and commonplace today among many White people. When confronted with their racial insensitivities, White politicians in both political parties have responded by insisting, "There is not a racist bone in my body."

As Robin DiAngelo, the author of *White Fragility: Why It's So Hard for White People to Talk About Racism*, has suggested, "The mainstream definition of 'racism' is when an individual consciously doesn't like people based on race and is intentionally mean to them. Who is going to own intentional meanness? That definition is the root of virtually all-White defensiveness."[1]

This attitude could be seen in President Trump's insistence that he's not a racist even when he claimed that the White supremacists who protested the removal of a Confederate statue in Charlottesville, Virginia, were good people just like the counter-protesters or when he suggested that the four women of Color in the House of Representatives in Congress who had publicly criticized his policies "should go back to where they came from." In his mind, these weren't racist comments, even though many believe they were. Adding to this White defensiveness is the current culture clash over the value of teaching our children about our nation's history of slavery and racism. This defensiveness can be seen in former President Trump's statement that "Critical race theory, the *1619 Project*, and the crusade against American history is toxic propaganda, ideological poison that, if not removed, will dissolve the civic bonds that tie us together." Many conservative Whites today simply don't want to be reminded of this history of racism and prefer to have a more positive history taught in our schools.

My experience engaging Whites in conversations about race has led me to agree with the writer Nadira Hira, who noted in her article, "Why the Fight Against Racism Has to Start with Owning It," there is a tendency among many White people to frame racism in terms of bad people doing bad things to people who aren't like them. Defining racism this way reduces White racial biases down to a mean-spirited dislike of People of Color and the use of intentionally discriminatory language and behavior. For many Whites, she claims, any discussion of possible racial biases, even philosophically, becomes an attack on our character. So, she says, "I may be hurt by something you've said or done, but bringing it to you automatically amounts to calling you a bad person, in effect making you the victim" rather than the other way around."[2]

White denial about the legacy of racism in America and the persistence of White racial biases is ubiquitous and firmly held by many, if not most, White people today. This can be readily seen in the way many of us frequently quibble about the meaning of words like racism, discrimination, and prejudice, often in a defensive manner. Yes, humans in many diverse cultures have long tended to develop racial and ethnic prejudices and stereotypes that reflect generalized ideas and beliefs about other people based on limited experiences or untested attitudes. And our personalized prejudices often serve to reinforce or justify preferences toward our own racial/ethnic group while categorizing other racial groups in negative ways. Some Whites like to justify this stereotyping of others as a "natural human tendency" that is devoid of real malice. White people often laugh at biased characterizations of others because we know they are exaggerated generalizations about people not like us. This can be seen in statements like "all Italians eat pasta and talk with their hands," "Asians all look alike," "all Southerners speak with a drawl and like country music," and "people who live in Minnesota love lutefisk." However, stereotyping groups of people by certain common traits they may share is not the same as holding prejudices that lead to discriminatory behavior aimed at elevating White people while diminishing the value, worth, or dignity of People of Color.

Secondly, many of us want to live with the illusion that the social, economic, educational, and political playing fields among racial groups in this country are now sufficiently leveled, and People of Color have been given equal opportunities for several decades. So, in their minds, most of the racial disparities or advantages that may exist today are not the fault of lingering White racial biases. As I noted earlier, this point of view is frequently cited by Whites, who point to a few African Americans who have managed to navigate successfully within the White-dominated world and have achieved prosperity or acclaim. In my local racial reconciliation work, I was challenged by an older White man to show our Courageous Conversations group a video produced by a conservative think tank entitled, "Where Are You, Martin Luther King?" In this video, a young, articulate African American man suggests that since the passage of civil rights legislation in the 1960s, the disparity gaps in wealth, incarceration rates, and educational achievements between Whites and Blacks in America have only become more pronounced. Like Sowell and O'Reilly, he insists that these achievement gaps are due to the failure of African Americans to take responsibility for their lives and to work to achieve their own success.

To his way of thinking, Affirmative Action policies and government-supported social welfare programs have been enough to overcome whatever handicaps People of Color have had from past racist actions on the part of Whites. Rather than acknowledging the impact that White racial biases may have had on People of Color, this form of White denial appeals to the ideology of an individual work ethic as the best way to address racial disparities that exist today. These White defensive perspectives on racial inequities completely miss the point of a Reagan-era political cartoon that depicted the president speaking to a large crowd about achieving economic success within the American free-market system. The president concludes his speech by saying, "So, let's all pull up our bootstraps and enjoy the prosperity that is within our reach." In the front row of the crowd, there is a Black teenager looking down at his bare feet.

Lastly, White denial today can be seen in the defensive pushback from Whites about the idea we enjoy some measure of White privilege that People of Color do not. This form of defensiveness overlooks the fact that a disproportionate number of People of Color end up in prison for essentially the same crimes as White people simply because they did not have access to the resources needed to ameliorate the punishments handed out in the criminal justice system. We discount the fact that Children of Color disproportionately face harsher punishments, suspensions, and expulsions for misbehavior at school than White children do. Whites often seek to rationalize the disparities and inequities in wealth, education, health, and access to power that exist between

Whites, Latinos, and African Americans by pointing out family system instabilities or the lack of self-discipline as "problems" inherent in communities of Color.

There are, however, countless examples of the many ways that White people have been given preferential treatment over People of Color in hiring practices, homeownership policies, and law enforcement stops, just to name a few. Some of the more notable of these have been reported in the racial profiling of People of Color by law enforcement agencies across the nation, which has become almost commonplace. The higher conviction and incarceration rates of People of Color in our criminal justice systems are now being seen as the result of poor legal defenses due to a lack of financial resources on the part of the defendant along with tough on crime policies. There are many less well-known cases of how White racial biases function and have been perpetuated for years, like the following report in a *New York Times* article in 1974:

"(Gross Pointe, Michigan) is the place where, until the nineteen-sixties, there was an operational point system whereby prospective residents were graded on such items as dress and swarthiness, and whether or not they were typically American. To be sold a home, Greeks, Italians and Jews had to earn more points than Anglo-Saxons. Blacks and Orientals could earn no points. When Grosse Pointe's first two Black residents moved in eight years ago (both have since followed their jobs out of the Detroit area), one was greeted by carloads of jeering Whites hurling racial insults."[3]

It should be noted here that Gross Point, Michigan, at that time, was a relatively affluent community made up mainly of educated White people. This example also demonstrates that White racial biases have not been confined to the South or ignorant people.

Despite all the contemporary evidence about the existence and perseverance of the idea of White superiority and White privilege in America today, most of us do not recognize how infected our souls and our society have become with these White preferential biases. So, we end up equivocating about the extent to which White identity continues to be of great value to most of us who have White skin, or we resist believing that Whites still enjoy numerous social and economic benefits that are not extended to People of Color. This denial process about our White identity takes many forms.

There is, first of all, the tendency among some of us to make evaluative distinctions between unacceptable expressions of White superiority and the more acceptable expressions of White social and cultural preferences. This can be seen in the recent decision by Facebook to stop making distinctions about the content of White identity speech on their social media platform. Facebook had initially banned White supremacist content from its platforms but maintained a murky distinction between White supremacy, White nationalism, and White separatism. In March 2019, however, the company noted that its views had been changed by civil society groups and experts in race relations. So, the company said it now believes White nationalism and separatism cannot be meaningfully distinguished from White supremacy and organized hate groups. This slow progress in coming to terms with the destructiveness of White racial bias and identities in society today reveals how White denial and discomfort with racial issues continue to evade a great deal of our White thinking and self-understanding.

Another form of White denial about the impact of racial biases on People of Color shows up in White claims of ignorance and not hearing or knowing about racial injustices. Some of this White denial is rooted in the way our nation's history of racial injustices has been sanitized or buried. There should be no doubt that much of American history has been written from the White point of view and to celebrate the heroes and accomplishments of White people of European ancestry. Consequently, the historical events and experiences impacting People of Color have been minimized and essentially left out of America's story. So, it should not be surprising to hear Whites claiming ignorance about how White racial biases have consistently shaped race relations and economic, political, and social policies in America over the past four hundred years.

I call this version of denial "White innocence." The fact that many Whites live in all-White social contexts and have little or no direct contact or associations with People of Color often leads to a general lack of awareness about racial inequities or race problems that non-White racial groups experience. From this "out of sight/out of mind" environment, many Whites who lead racially sheltered lives simply have no personal experiences or existential reasons to be concerned about racial issues or injustices simply because such issues never really impact most of us who are White. This White isolationism creates a benign type of White unfamiliarity with and indifference to racial biases that negatively impact People of Color. Not only has this racial-awareness innocence kept many Whites from noticing or being concerned about racism, but it also can shield us from taking any responsibility for addressing our own racial biases or those of other Whites.

It actually seems disingenuous to me, given all the media attention that race issues have received over the past forty or more years, that White innocence about racial justice and equity issues still gets expressed. This amounts to thinking that "if the problem doesn't affect me, then there's no problem." This attitude conveniently overlooks the fact that historians have been recounting for decades now events and experiences like the slave trade, the fracture of our nation over the slavery issues, the injustices of the Jim Crow era, and the struggles of the civil rights movement. White denial may explain why the teaching of American history has avoided mentioning the genocide of the Native American populations by White Europeans in order to claim their indigenous land, or the enslavement of Africans for cheap labor, or the continued oppression of People of Color after the passage of the Thirteenth, Fourteenth, and Fifteenth Amendments to the U.S. Constitution, or the continued use of power and domination by White citizens to terrorize and oppress People of Color in the name of White superiority. Such historical acknowledgments are difficult in themselves because this "truth-telling" contradicts the kind of American exceptionalism that most of us have been taught in school and that continues to be promoted today among those who claim they want to "make America great again."

Our White orientation to our nation's history is evident in the stories and narratives that focus almost exclusively on the achievements, institutions, courageous adventures, and heroic stories of White people who gave shape to this nation. This racial filtering is particularly noticeable in the contemporary allegiance that many White southerners give to the Lost Cause narrative about the origins and impact of the Civil War. Those who want to preserve this Southern narrative reject the fact that Confederate monuments were erected all over the South during the Jim Crow era to reinforce White superiority. They want to claim these racist monuments are only memorials to loyal soldiers who fought for the Confederacy, like any other war veteran memorial and represent "Southern heritage" that needs to be honored and preserved.

I can understand this desire to protect family heritage and pride. My great-grandfather fought in the Confederate army. On his tombstone in a small cemetery near Stone Mountain, Georgia, along with his name and the dates of his birth and death, is a large inscription that notes he was a soldier in the Confederate States of America, Georgia Regiment 1. However, I can acknowledge that my great-grandfather was morally on the wrong side in the Civil War without needing to defend my family heritage.

The persistence of White denial today about the ugliness and contradictions of racism in America's history is apparent in the debates about whether or not to continue to give Confederate monuments civic places of honor in our communities. The same can be said about the debates going on now about policy decisions to prevent the teaching of critical race theory in schools.

From my perspective, the attempts by some southerners to claim that Confederate monuments only pay tribute to faithful soldiers who were largely not slaveholders and who fought for states' rights is an effort to deny the racist mindset that created these memorials at the height of the Jim Crow era. The mythological claim that the Civil War was fought on behalf of states' rights begs the question of what rights the Southern states that left the Union wanted to maintain. The competing perspectives about our racist national history were documented by a 2011 Pew Research Center poll that revealed 48 percent of Americans today believe the Civil War was mainly about "states' rights," while only 38 percent of us believe the main cause was the issue of slavery. Deeper causes for the Civil War, like the belief in White superiority among the races, did not even get considered in the polling. The ideology of White superiority as a cause of the Civil War has rarely been acknowledged in most of our American history books. This in itself is telling given that most of the declarations of secession made by the Southern states that joined the Confederacy in 1860–61 made White supremacy a key issue for their secession.

Listen, for example, to how the convention delegates who developed the 1861 Texas Ordinance of Secession identified their reasons for joining the Confederacy: "We hold as undeniable truths that the governments of the various States, and of the confederacy itself, were established exclusively by the White race, for themselves and their posterity, that the African race had no agency in their establishment, that they were rightfully held and regarded as an inferior and dependent race, and in that condition only could their existence in this country be rendered beneficial or tolerable."[4]

This devotion to Southern pride in remembering and celebrating the Civil War reveals the hubris that resides in the desire to protect our White virtues and heritage. Even more troubling, this White defense has also included the twisted notion that slavery wasn't that bad because African American ancestors "were born the slaves of barbarian masters, untaught in the useful arts and occupations, reared in heathen darkness, and, sold by heathen masters, they were transferred to shores enlightened by the rays of Christianity."[5]

As the Yale historian David Blight points out in his seminal book on this subject, the "die-hard" Lost Cause narrative was picked up by the likes of the United Daughters of the Confederacy who went so far as to claim that "Negroes under the institution of slavery were well-fed, well-clothed, and well-housed," and they were thus far better off than what they had experienced in the Reconstruction period.[6]

Few White people seem to know or care about the violence and oppression that African Americans suffered during the Jim Crow era when Confederate monuments were erected in the early decades of the twentieth century, and the KKK terrorized Black people. We turn a blind eye today to the White ideological values promoted in Thomas Dixon's epic 1905 story, *The Clansman*, that D.W. Griffith turned into the blockbuster 1915 movie *Birth of a Nation,* which President Wilson showed in the White House. It's difficult to understand why so many White people seem to ignore this history or to minimize its relevance to the legacy of racism today. Even today, state legislatures are enacting laws to prevent the teaching of critical race theory in public schools. The goal seems to be aimed at protecting White students from uncomfortable historical facts and to preserve the idea of American moral exceptionalism. I see both of these efforts as manifestations of our White denial about the distasteful legacy of racism.

I am among those who believe a close examination of the collective history of these United States of America that pays attention to how People of Color have been treated and portrayed is a vital step in recognizing and coming to terms with the ubiquity of our White racial biases today. Thankfully, academic historians and sociologists alike have produced plenty of honest portraits of our nation's history regarding the dynamics of White racial biases. Historian Eric Foner has identified the earliest forms of racism in America as "the tiny seed of poisoned fruit" that arrived in 1619 on a Dutch ship that brought twenty African men and women to these shores as enslaved persons.[7]

In many respects, we have only begun in the past several decades to publicly recognize and acknowledge in our predominately White society the uncomfortable, ugly, and regrettable history of the genocide, the chattel slavery, the Jim Crow laws, and the White resistance to racial equality during the civil rights era. Most White students like me never heard in our history classes anything about the so-called race riots, as labeled by Whites, or more accurately described as race massacres by historians that took place from the Civil War period right up into the 1960s. Most Whites have little knowledge or understanding of the angry White mob violence that led to the murdering of countless Blacks and the burning of their homes in places like Tulsa, Oklahoma, in 1921 or Rosewood, Florida, in 1923, or East St. Louis in 1917, or Chicago in 1919, or Elaine, Arkansas, in 1918.

The only race riot we learned about was the Nat Turner Slave Rebellion in Virginia that created a panic within the White communities prior to the Civil War. The White racial violence against innocent Blacks that stretches from Colfax, Louisiana, in 1873 to Orangeburg, South Carolina, in 1968 has been all but buried. Here in Texas, the 1910 Slocum Massacre in which Blacks were viciously killed and their land was stolen rarely gets mentioned in this state's history. The same is true about the 261 lynchings of African Americans that took place in Texas.

After a number of race riots in Detroit and Los Angeles in the 1960s, President Johnson appointed a special commission to study the issues and problems that had led to those racial tragedies. As historian Jill Lepore points out about the White conservative viewpoint expressed at that time, William F. Buckley, Jr. wrote, "What caused the riots isn't segregation or poverty or frustration. What caused them is a psychological disorder which is tearing at the ethos of our society as a result of boredom, self-hatred, and the arrogant contention that all our shortcomings are the result of other people's aggressions upon us." Simply put, when Whites like Buckley encountered Black resistance to the abuses of power and racial injustices by Whites, they tried to blame People of Color for creating the environment that resulted in racial tensions and problems. It has only been in the last decade or so that we have now begun to recognize the persistence of racial discrimination in law enforcement rather than argue that most People of Color have a penchant for criminal activity.

Despite our efforts to ignore or sanitize our nation's racist history, a number of efforts have been made in recent years to address openly and honestly our troubled past with racial injustices. Historians are now writing about America's history from the point of view of the victims of racial violence and oppression (see, for example, Howard Zinn's *A People's History of the United States*, or *Slave Nation: How Slavery United the Colonies and Sparked the*

American Revolution by Alfred, Ruth, and Steven Blumrosen, or *Lone Star Pasts: Memory and History in Texas*, edited by Gregg Cantrell and Elizabeth Hayes Turner). Documentaries on forgotten or buried events in our racial history have received wide attention. In recent years several museums and memorials have opened to tell the stories publicly of People of Color and their resilience to White racism, including the National Museum of African American History and Culture in Washington, DC, The National Memorial to Peace and Justice and the Enslavement Museum in Montgomery, Alabama, and the National Civil Rights Museum in Memphis, Tennessee. Many of us have gained a greater awareness of and appreciation for the racial plight of People of Color in our nation's history from visiting these memorials and museums. While visiting these museums and memorials is often painful and embarrassing for many White Americans, these collections of our unspoken national history provide the needed awareness for White people to work on what Bryan Stevenson, the founder of the Equal Justice Initiative, has called our "White empathy deficit."

My more recent experiences engaging in conversations about race have led me to recognize that a large measure of White denial about the pervasiveness of White racial bias resides in both our lack of empathy for the targets of our racial biases and the desire to defend our racial identity. It astonishes me how often some White people will claim that People of Color have enjoyed the same opportunities and rights that White people have since the passage of civil rights legislation in the 1960s. In their minds, a generation or two of equal rights have effectively erased twenty generations of White racial oppression that subjected African Americans to the brutality of chattel slavery, the injustices of Jim Crow segregation, and the psychological and social humiliation and degradation from being treated as inferior people. Many White people seem to have more empathy for abused animals, military veterans, and recovering alcoholics than they do for Native Americans, African Americans, and Mexican Americans or anyone else who has been routinely and continuously subjected to White racial biases and abuse for centuries now in America.

I can only surmise why so many White people in this country rarely express much empathy for the racial sins of the past. Some of this empathy deficit may simply be the result of wanting to think the best about ourselves and not be implicated in the racial injustices in our nation's history. Many White people have bought into our national narrative about American exceptionalism and prefer to remember our "better angels" rather than acknowledge our country's moral imperfections. For generations, Western European cultures have claimed that non-White cultures of the world are inferior and need to be civilized and improved by Whites. Some of this thinking persists in ways not easily recognized. In the recording of American history, the accomplishments and triumphs of this experiment in democracy are attributed to the dominant White population, while the genocidal, racist, sexist, and nefarious historical behaviors of Whites have been largely left out or ignored. Slowly, White America has been awakening in recent years from this dreaming White innocence about our nation's history. A growing willingness has emerged in recent years among historians and social critics who want to tell the unvarnished truth about the good, the bad, and the ugly in our collective national identity and formation. Nevertheless, many White people have difficulty facing the truth about how our dominant racial group in America has repeatedly dehumanized non-Whites while elevating our own racial heritage. I believe our collective White acknowledgment of our racist history has to be part of our efforts to achieve racial reconciliation in America's future.

Ironically, many of the more truthful voices about the legacy of our White racial biases have been available to us for ages, although ignored up until recently. On his otherwise appreciative visit to the United States in the 1830s, Alexis de Tocqueville noted that the prejudices of the Whites against the Blacks seemed to increase in proportion as slavery was being abolished. In his keen observations about the American experiment in the New World, he claimed, "There is a natural prejudice which prompts men to despise whomsoever has been their inferior, long after he has become their equal, and the real inequality which is produced by fortune or by law, is always succeeded by an imaginary inequality which is implanted in the manners of the people."[8]

In commenting on the threat that the racial divide presented for the future of the United States before the Civil War, Tocqueville made this prediction: "To induce the Whites to abandon the opinion they have conceived of the moral and intellectual inferiority of their former slaves, the negroes must change; but as long as this opinion subsists, to change is impossible."

As the historian David Brion Davis has pointed out, the dominant White histories of slavery in America into the twentieth century, like Ulrich Phillips' unapologetically racist book, *American Negro Slavery* (1918), affirmed that Blacks were "inferior to Whites and that southern slavery has been a benign civilizing force for easy-going, amiable . . . sturdy light-hearted savages from Africa."[9]

Racist views about the threat that People of Color posed to the idea of White supremacy were certainly not confined to the South. The educational and academic defense for these racist views was promoted by the Harvard-educated historian and journalist who wrote several books advocating for eugenics and "scientific racism" (see *The Rising Tide of Color Against White World-Supremacy*, Lothrop Stoddard).

To confront and eradicate White racial biases today requires a commitment and willingness to recognize how profoundly America has been racialized by White people from its beginning. This includes recognition and acceptance of the fact that the typical history of the United States of America have been told mainly from the White vantage point. The significance and impact of White racial biases in the history of America has usually been left out in the story of the development of this nation. Rarely do we hear that racism in America first appeared when Western Europeans arrived in the New World to colonize this land by committing genocide against the native indigenous peoples who were living here under the claim that they were "savages."

Many of us did not learn how the Constitution of the United States of America was carefully constructed around White racist ideas. Even though slavery was the precipitating cause of the Civil War, most histories do not say that this "peculiar institution" was based on beliefs about White superiority. Most of us did not learn how White racism gave rise to the Chinese Exclusion Act in the late nineteenth century.

Even as a history major in college, I do not recall learning about the reign of terror that White vigilantes known as the Ku Klux Klan and even the Texas Rangers carried out for decades against People of Color. When the history of the civil rights movement gets addressed, very little is said about how White racism led to the bombing of African American churches or the use violence to counter peaceful protests by Blacks seeking voting rights or wanting to be served in restaurants. Students in high school rarely hear that the foundational belief in this national racialized history is the notion of clearly defined racial hierarchies that were legitimized politically, socially, educationally, and religiously by White people for two hundred years. The significance that racism has played in

American history appears to have been sanitized or overlooked for the sake of glorifying our dominant White history. The perpetuation of this historical amnesia about how racial biases have shaped our nation is an aspect of White denial that we need to move beyond to achieve a new commitment to racial equality and justice.

I could give many examples, of course, to illustrate how the idea of racial hierarchies and White superiority have been used to devalue the humanity of People of Color, to prevent non-Whites from achieving equal opportunities under the law, and to perpetuate racial injustices in American history. For the sake of brevity, I will only give one example that reveals the dynamics of how the White commitment to preserving the belief in White superiority among the races has shaped our nation. This can easily be seen in the crisis that took place in 1957 when nine Black teenagers attempted to integrate Central High School in Little Rock, Arkansas. In 1954, the Supreme Court had ruled in the *Brown v. Board of Education* case that racial segregation in the nation's public schools did not represent separate but equal education. This legal decision at the federal level threatened to undo the segregated school systems in Southern states. Local school districts were compelled to develop school integration plans to comply with the federal desegregation ruling.

In reaction to this federal educational mandate, the Little Rock School Board, the governor of the state, and the local White community sought to fight this federal move to racially integrate their schools. The White citizens made it clear that they wanted to maintain the White racial hierarchy that had long existed in the region. As the nation watched, the governor of Arkansas ordered National Guard troops to prevent nine eligible Black high school students from entering Central High School as a large mob of angry Whites jeered and heckled the students as they attempted to attend the school. A week later, President Eisenhower ordered

Army troops to protect the students so they could enroll at the previously all-White high school.

News reports about the governor's attempts to block school integration in Little Rock, along with the vile reactions of the White protesters, were communicated to the rest of the nation on television and in newspapers. The racist behavior of the angry Whites toward these students of color demonstrated how deeply attached White southerners were to maintaining a racially segregated society based on the belief in White superiority and Black inferiority. The resentment of Whites around the South was intensified when the federal government showed that these Whites could no longer depend on the law to support their racial hierarchy. Lest we forget the inhumanity and the violence that often accompanied the integration of public schools in America, I recommend a visit to the National Parks Interpretative Center at Central High School in Little Rock. The pictures and the stories of what took place there in 1957 will help illuminate for any visitor the sad dynamics of this ardent White allegiance to maintaining White racial superiority.

My experience with White denial about racial issues has been reinforced by African Americans like journalist Leonard Pitts who frequently hears pushback from Whites on articles he writes about racial justice issues in the news today. As he notes, "There are few things harder than to get some White people to wrestle with or even concede—their racial assumptions and privilege. There is no asininity they will not embrace, no rationalization they will not employ, no illogic they will not apply, to avoid confronting how racist America was—and still is."

As Pitts often points out from everyday stories about White discrimination, generations of Black Americans know that their education level, where they live, what they've achieved, or how affluent they are, does not matter as much as the color of their skin when they encounter White people. Pitts states candidly that their experience tells them that White people often weaponize dark skin as a source of fear and inequality of character. Yet, White people constantly insist that "we" have BIPOC friends, or we make the audacious claim that we are "color-blind." Rather than acknowledging the negative judgments White people often make about non-Whites, most Whites go to great lengths to claim we are exceptional and do not harbor *any* White racial biases. People of Color simply know better from their experiences with Whites.

White denial about our racial biases comes in many forms, including the accusation that Blacks and other non-Whites often play "the race card" in order to avoid taking responsibility for their own well-being. Tim Wise, the long-time White activist for racial reconciliation, has examined the "playing the race card" accusation, and he calls into question why anyone would want to play this card, especially since the card is often ineffective. Even if some People of Color do play the "race card," Wise compellingly contends that *White people play the White denial card even more frequently*. Whites have always doubted People of Color when they claim that racism exists. This is why playing the race card is usually futile. White people, Wise notes, often continue to deny the racial aspects of incidents even when they are compelled to recognize the strong evidence that is produced before them. Wise concludes that "whatever 'card' claims of racism may prove to be for the Black and Brown, the denial card is far away from the trump card, and Whites play it regularly."

Consequently, I believe that dismantling racism in America requires Whites to stop denying or dismissing how we all have been implicated in this history of racial biases. Racism is taught and learned, both individually and collectively. And the ideology of White superiority continues to operate in American society in more ways than most of us who are White want to acknowledge.

The hatred and violence that often emanates from White racism against People of Color are as shocking and horrific when it shows up today as it was during the Jim Crow lynching era.

Let me offer one example. On a Saturday night in 1998, three White men were riding around Jasper, Texas, when they came upon James Byrd, Jr., a forty-nine-year-old Black man, who was walking home after drinking with friends. The driver of the truck, Shawn Allen Berry, offered Mr. Byrd a ride. At some point during the night, the three attacked James Byrd, spray-painted his face, then used a logging chain to tie him to the rear bumper of the truck. They drove along Huff Creek Road, an isolated path lined thick with pine and sweet gum trees, for three miles as Mr. Byrd was helplessly flung side to side. His naked body, brutalized, dismembered, and discarded, was found in front of a Black cemetery just outside Jasper. As a newspaper report noted, the motive seemed shockingly clear-cut: One of the perpetrators, John William King, who had come out of a stint in prison, was a committed White supremacist and his body was a billboard of racist tattoos, including one depicting a Black man hanging in a noose.

As disturbing and horrific as this act of racist violence is for many of us to comprehend, there are tens of thousands, if not a million or more, White people in America who firmly believe that their White identity and culture are being threatened simply by the presence of People of Color living among us. Ironically, it is often racially conscious People of Color like Kamau Bell, host of the TV documentary *The United Shades of America*, who seek to bring attention to these ardent White racists most of us seek to minimize. White denial about our nation's legacy of racism has been front and center recently with conservative politicians seeking to pass laws to prevent Confederate monuments from being removed from public places of honor, the suppression of voting rights for People of Color, and preventing schoolteachers from exposing their students to America's tragic racist history. Instead of acknowledging or examining how racial identity has shaped our nation's history and policies, the goal of these legal actions appears to be to an effort to deny any responsibility or complicity in maintaining White racial biases.

There are, of course, honest Whites who can acknowledge both our nation's racist history and the fact that individual and institutional racial biases still exist today within the White community. But even then, many of us affirm this reality at an intellectual and philosophical level but not at an emotional or personal level. This personal distancing from racial biases sometimes represents in itself a form of White denial. The denial occurs when we imagine ourselves as being socially informed about the history of racial discrimination and morally evolved but have not addressed our latent fears about People of Color or recognize how our White privilege contributes to racial disparities or expectations. This intellectual embracing of the misguided dynamics of White racism often allows some of us to avoid an examination of how we are implicated in the economic, social, and political dimensions of White privilege or how our biases impact our relationships or lack of with People of Color. Consequently, it is not uncommon for educated and ethically grounded White people to raise their voices on behalf of the racially oppressed and to scold the overt racists while doing little or nothing to address the poverty of our own relationships with People of Color.

Dismantling racism in America requires all of us to confront the various forms of White denial and White innocence about how our racial biases are ingrained in our shared history and continue to play out in racial experiences to this day. I believe that getting beyond all the evasions we make regarding our widely shared implicit and embedded racial biases begins when we can stop trying to preserve the virtues we attach to being "White" or quit being ignorant about the presence of racism. For many of us, this kind of denial about and resistance to acknowledging the presence of White racial biases is a huge challenge we must face, confess, and overcome before we are ready to work on liberating ourselves from them.

CHAPTER FOUR
UNPACKING THE COMPLEXITY OF WHITE RACISM

"Most Whites in America in 1967, including many persons of goodwill, proceed from a premise that equality is a loose expression for improvement. White America is not even psychologically organized to close the gap- essentially it seeks only to make it less painful and less obvious but in most respects to retain it."

—Martin Luther King, Jr.

The importance that White people in America have historically attached to a person's skin color encompasses a complicated and sordid history. Some of this history, of course, can be traced back to the enslavement of Africans for economic benefits by White plantation owners and merchants during the pre-Civil War era in the U.S.. Even before the African slave trade, however, the so-called native (Red-skinned) people of the Americas were de-monized, exploited, and murdered by White European settlers in the formative years of the United States of America to steal their land and to devalue their indigenous cultures all in the name of religion, establishing a new nation based on democracy, and a higher form of human civilization.

After the Emancipation of African slaves during the Civil War, White racial biases against non-Whites certainly did not end. As Douglas Blackmon has documented in his Pulitzer Prize–winning book, *Slavery by Another Name: The Re-Enslavement of Black Americans from the Civil War to World War II,* the continued White subjugation and oppression of African Americans in post-Civil War America was institutionalized with Jim Crow–era laws that extended racial discrimination to include brown-skinned Latinos, and the so-called yellow skin Asians via the Chinese Exclusion Act for more than another one hundred years. These embedded White racial biases were reinforced by "separate but equal" court rulings, with miscegenation laws against interracial marriages, with public school segregation, with the redlining of neighborhoods to deny home loans to People of Color in the twentieth-century housing industry, and with unequal U.S. criminal justice and immigration policies into the twenty-first century.

Many Whites today seem to have forgotten or never learned how the dominant White society in America has long used skin color as a marker for social, economic, and political acceptability and access. The significance that a person's skin color represents has even been inverted within minority racial groups, as Ibram Kendi has noted among African Americans who embraced the Black pride notion that darker skin is more beautiful and desired than light-skinned Blacks.[1]

When it comes to racial identities in America, there has long been one basic reality: Those of us who are White enjoy being among the predominant and valued "race" in this country. It is simply easy for us to forget about our skin color on a day-to-day basis. This isn't the case for People of Color. As the African

American writer Toni Morrison has pointed out, "In this country *American* means White. Everybody else has to hyphenate."

For a host of reasons, our predominantly White nation has a long history of identifying people living here according to the social and cultural construct of "race." Historians and sociologists today point out that "race" is a social and psychological category created by White people of European descent to categorize people on the basis of skin color and other physical attributes. Regardless of the professed political and religious ideas about human equality and freedom, Whites in America have attached great meaning to the differences in skin color tones of people, thereby suggesting that our human differences are somehow more than "skin deep."

In our dominant White culture, we have often labeled people from a variety of ancestries and ethnicities according to skin colors and a few other physical attributes. During my lifetime, for instance, the White community has changed the acceptable racial categories for dark-skinned people from "Negro" to "Colored" to "Black" to "African American;" and for brown-skinned people from "Mexican" to "Hispanic" to "Brown" to "Latino." We have done the same with Native Americans ("Redskins," "Indians," "Indigenous Peoples") and with Asians ("Orientals," "Yellow"). Even more telling are the derogatory terms we have given to non-White people to suggest they are somehow less human or capable than White people: "niggers," "wet-backs," "chinks," "savages," etc. This long-standing White habit of identifying and demeaning non-Whites reveals a strange psychological need among White-skinned people to claim both racial and cultural superiority over darker-skinned people. Let's not forget that White segregationists in this country have always worried about maintaining "White racial purity" and preventing possible biological and cultural contamination from People of Color.

Without knowing much about racial history in the United States of America, most Whites can easily and innocently overlook the far-reaching impact that "systemic racism" has had on People of Color. **Systemic racism is the recognition of systems and structures embedded in society developed by the complex interactions of White culture, public policies, and institutional practices that create disadvantages, disparities, and injustices for People of Color.** As Joe Feagin points out in his book *Systemic Racism: A Theory of Oppression*, White racial biases and discriminatory practices against People of Color in America's history have had what we might call a cumulative effect, or what he calls the "social generation of oppression." From the outset, European colonizers practiced a predatory ethic of claiming the lands and labor of non-Whites, created economic structures that benefited Whites but not non-Whites, maintained cultural imperialism and political power imbalance that favored Whites while oppressing People of Color. These structural aspects of racism were predicated on notions about White superiority attributed to natural law or Christian ideas about evangelizing the heathen. Consequently, the pervasive and socially ingrained White racial biases over time have led to most of the racial inequities and inequalities we see in America today. For anyone who wants to learn how systemic racism has functioned in America, Feagin's book offers numerous examples and research studies to support this understanding.

So, it should not be surprising to any of us today that contemporary racial surveys reveal there is still a strong social and cultural preference in our country toward being "White." When people of varying races are asked about their desire to change their skin color, if we could, most White people respond by saying they do not want to have a different skin color. Many People of Color, however, realize the benefits that would come to them if they were White skinned. For all of today's insistence that we are and should be a "color-blind" society, most of us know that skin color still makes a big difference in how people are perceived and treated.

Jane Elliot, the educator who used differences in eye color to teach her White students about racial discrimination, would ask White high school and college students sitting in an auditorium to stand up if they would change skin color if they could with Black people. When no one in the audience stood up, she would repeat the inquiry again, saying that maybe they didn't understand the instruction. When none of the students indicated they would want to change their skin color, Elliot suggested that this was evidence itself that they knew that their White identity provided them with advantages over People of Color.

Adding to this complexity of racial biases in America has been the White tendency to frame racism as a problem for People of Color rather than as a problem that White people have. In terms of obtaining racial equality, Whites have often talked about what People of Color can or should do to improve their lives and to escape racial biases. As long as we see the problems of racism residing with People of Color and not with those of us who are White, we will argue that "they" need to see the value of education, and obeying the law, and staying married to raise children, etc. Moreover, White people often want to treat the symptoms of racism that non-Whites suffer from rather than address the root causes within the White community.

So, White progressives advocate for measures like Head Start programs, charity outreach to the poor, and reducing recidivism rates in the criminal justice system, etc. On the whole, most Whites today think we can eradicate racial injustices by giving People of Color more opportunities or find ways to close the economic wealth gaps between the races or ensuring that law enforcement and the criminal justice system treat People of Color more fairly.

While these efforts are certainly needed, Whites rarely get around to addressing how our embedded racial biases, along with systemic racism, create inequities between People of Color and us. Some of us also choose to dismiss the impact of generations of racial biases by arguing that the more critical issues impacting People of Color today have more to do with social or economic class than with skin color. Surveys indicate that younger generations of Whites often tend to think that economics play more of a central role in racial inequities and injustices than racial identities.

In listening to those who reduce race issues down to social and economic class issues, I can appreciate the observation that race and class are deeply intertwined in American society today. There is little doubt that economics has played a significant role in race relations in our nation's history. However, by recognizing the systemic nature of White racial biases, we are better able to see how White economic interests have actually shaped much of the history of racism in our nation.

In many respects, the racial inequities and injustices that we can point to today are manifested in both economic disparities and social class issues that exist in our communities. The dynamics of race at a systemic level can be seen in the differences in wealth accumulation, access to good educational resources, uneven health care, opportunities to obtain affordable housing and living-wage jobs, and a host of other factors that give advantages to Whites while negatively impacting People of Color.

The remnants of social segregation and cultural attitudes that we sometimes associate with racial identities conspire together to create what Isabelle Wilkerson has called America's version of a "caste" hierarchy. One of the dimensions of systemic White racial biases that we should address here is around the assumption that eradicating individual implicit biases will bring about more racial equity and put an end to racial injustices. This viewpoint overlooks the extent to which structural and institutional White racial biases are embedded in the fabric of American culture and how White privilege functions to give certain advantages to Whites that People of Color often do not receive. As Ibram Kendi has pointed out in his book on becoming an anti-racist, putting an end to race-based advantages and disadvantages requires a commitment to address public policies that lead to racial inequities and to replace such policies with more equitable institutional practices. But to do so, I believe, requires White people to recognize how our White culture has used non-White skin color to marginalize People of Color economically, socially, and politically for generations while White skin color has benefitted those of us who are White. There is no doubt that creating job opportunities for all people, ensuring equal access to a good education and to adequate health care, and providing affordable housing for everyone will benefit our entire nation and lessen the racial disparities we see today. However, White racial biases within our nation's institutions will still have to be addressed before racial equity can be achieved in America.

The economic and educational conditions of People of Color in this country are sometimes seen by White people as being more critical to troubled race relations than the idea of White superiority or racial discrimination. Jacqueline Jones argues along these lines in *A Dreadful Deceit: The Myth of Race from the Colonial Era to Obama's America.* This point of view is similar to W. E. B. DuBois' theory in his 1940 book *Dusk of Dawn: An Essay Toward an Autobiography of a Race Concept.* While DuBois welcomed multiracial working-class solidarity, he maintained that many oppressed Whites were strongly attached to their "Whiteness" as a marker of status, even though it brought them few or no material advantages. Jones contends that racial justifications for unequal treatment have served the economic benefits of Whites and stand as self-serving lies to keep Blacks in a cheap labor pool. DuBois, however, emphasized that those who accept racist thinking are generally self-deceived and buy into mystifying fiction about economic success. Even though DuBois was no less concerned about Black economic disadvantages than Jones, DuBois worried as well about the self-contempt that racial defamation causes. Material well-being without self-respect, he insisted, is an undignified existence.

Since distinctions in social and economic status can be found among Whites as well as People of Color, it does seem that factors like inherited wealth, access to higher education, and social respect have a profound impact on the lives of people regardless of their racial identity. Poverty creates class distinctions among those who we might call "marginalized" people simply because they do not enjoy all the benefits that some measure of wealth brings to others of us. However, while race is certainly a social construction, it has real material consequences for those living in this country. The fact that nationwide significantly larger proportions of People of Color are incarcerated in the criminal justice system, have poorer health and less access to health care, face higher levels of unemployment, are less likely to get a higher education all to suggest that race does matter even when we might say that class differences matter more. So, racial identities often transcend social or economic class. This can be seen in the social competition and the animosity that so-called redneck White people often express toward African Americans, Latinos, and those of Asian descent.

According to data collected in the 2009 census, White people are substantially less likely to live under poverty than People of Color (the official poverty rate is 9.4 percent for non-Hispanic White people and 25.8 for Black people). Of course, being White in itself does not guarantee material success in this country.

Racial categorizations influence but are by no means the primary determinant of wealth or privilege. There are hosts of successful African Americans and Latinos in our nation today who have not been limited by their racial heritage. But few of them will say their racial identification helped them in their achievements. Most had to work around the ways that their racial identity represented an obstacle they had to overcome in a predominately White society. And along racial lines, the wealth gap has been obvious. According to an analysis of Federal Reserve data by the Urban Institute several years ago, the median net worth of Black families was only $11,030 as compared with $134,230 for Whites.

The complexity of racial biases in this country also comes up today when some Whites actually complain about "reverse discrimination" against White people. To this way of thinking, anti-racial discrimination and equal opportunity laws have now created a form of racism against White-skinned people. It's always fascinating and ironic to me to hear Whites complain about "racial discrimination" when governments, educational institutions, or corporations attempt to implement some racial balancing and inclusion provisions in their hiring, admissions, or promotion practices. For whatever reason, many of us have been less bothered or outraged by racial discrimination when it impacts People of Color.

Several years ago, the Public Religion Research Institute conducted a poll of adults aged eighteen to twenty-four on topics from religion and morality to economic issues and the 2012 election. This survey also asked questions on race and ethnicity: Does the government pay too much attention to the problems of Blacks and other minorities? Is "reverse discrimination" a problem in today's society? Is demographic change a good thing for American society? Nearly half of the respondents said that the government pays too much attention to the problems of minorities, while 48 percent also agree that discrimination against Whites is a genuine problem. Even more surprising are the responses from younger White millennials. It is disconcerting to me to learn that 56 percent of millennials say that the government has paid too much attention to the problems of Blacks and other minorities. Among younger Whites, 58 percent say that "discrimination against Whites has become as big a problem as discrimination against Blacks and other minorities." Despite generations of racism against People of Color, there is a mystifying notion among some Whites today that the gains made for People of Color have resulted in losses for those of us who are White. These White feelings and perceptions only add to the complexity of racial biases in America today.

Many African Americans, however, think this belief in reverse discrimination against White people is distorted if not ridiculous. As one Black writer has said,

> *If you are White in the United States, almost everyone in a position of power or influence looks like you. You won't be questioned if you find yourself in a nice part of town, you won't be the picture of criminality, and few people will ever question your right to take government help. Cops won't give you a hard time as a matter of course, and no one will ask you to speak for White people as a whole. Sports fans won't go apoplectic and shower you with racial slurs because you scored a goal (or kneel during the National Anthem). The list goes on.[2]*

Some African American scholars suggest that White racial biases are shared by both political conservatives and liberals. As Ibram Kendi points out, a new vocabulary has emerged that allows the White establishment in all its variations to evade the charge of racism. He includes in his list terms like these: law and order, war on drugs, reverse discrimination, race-neutral, welfare queen, tough on crime, personal responsibility, Black-on-Black crime, achievement gap, race card, color-blind, post-racial, All Lives Matter, voter fraud, war on cops, Obamacare, etc. Kendi argues that both liberals and conservatives use terms like these to support their beliefs that People of Color are necessarily stuck in cycles of unstable families, criminal cultures, the deprivations of poverty, and low moral values.[3] Whether we use the terms "systemic," "structural," "institutional," or "cultural" to describe the pervasiveness of racial biases that Whites have used to our advantage while disadvantaging People of Color, our understanding of race in America must face the issue that Joseph Barndt points out in his comprehensive book *Understanding & Dismantling Racism: The Twenty-First Century Challenge To White America*. As he says, "Whatever else race is, it has always had something to do with determining who gets how much of what in any society, and it still does."

Another important element in unpacking the complexity of racism in America for most Whites centers on how our nation's history is told and celebrated by us. When it comes to racism, some often argue that our history books have been "sanitized" when it comes to how White racial attitudes and practices impacted People of Color in the development of this country. As a history major in college, I learned very little about the values, beliefs, and biases that undergirded to the institution of chattel slavery in America, or why non-Whites were considered to be three-fifths of a person in the original Constitution, and how People of Color were oppressed, terrorized, and marginalized from the plantation era all the way to the 1960s. In essence, People of Color did not play much of a role in American history other than being a "problem" at various times for Whites.

As Dr. William J. Gardiner writes about the history of White supremacy in the U.S., one of the important themes that played out in our history is how Whites became the "real" Americans. Consequently, White people have not seriously dealt with the fact that our ancestors took this continent from Native Americans who had been here for ten thousand years. The history of genocide and horrific White brutality toward People of Color has been effectively "Whitewashed" out of the narratives about America's success story and rise to world dominance. To portray Whites as the "real" Americans, a variety of justifications for the preeminent role of White domination have been used in the telling of our nation's story, including viewing White European colonists as being God's ordained people to inhabit this continent, the formulating of the Discovery Doctrine, promoting the idea of a Manifest Destiny, the appeals to Social Darwinism, and the assertion that the Native Americans have "disappeared."

In his book *The Invention of the White Race*, Theodore Allen describes how the racial formation process that was developed in Ireland set a precedent for the relationship between Africans and Europeans in the American colonies. The English treated the native people of Ireland as an inferior race in the six northern counties of Ulster. The English referred to the Irish as savages—just as they described the Native Americans later. In Ireland, loyal Scot settlers were made into a landlord class to provide social control over the Irish people using the Penal Laws of Protestant Ascendancy. The Penal Laws were the forerunners of the slave codes that were developed in the new American colonies. In the American colonies, a buffer social control group—like the Scots in Ireland—was needed to stand between the mass of slaves and the numerically tiny class of slaveholders. Allen writes, "The primary emphasis upon 'race' became the pattern only when the bourgeoisie could not form its social control apparatus without the inclusion of property less Euro-Americans."

During the American Revolution, White colonists had to confront the moral dilemma of fighting for political and economic freedom while, at the same time, murdering indigenous peoples and enslaving Africans. One colonization ideology rejected undemocratic divisions of class and ancestry, while another accepted unequal placement based on race. Consequently, when the U.S. Constitution was written, Black slaves amounted to only three-fifths of a person. Later, when an enslaved Negro sued to gain his freedom in a state where slavery was prohibited, the Supreme Court provided a sweeping legal opinion in 1857 that institutionalized White supremacy as the law of the land. The Dred Scott decision offered this disturbing yet binding racial opinion written by Chief Justice Roger Taney: Enslaved African Americans "had for more than a century before been regarded as beings of an inferior order, and altogether unfit to associate with the white race, either in social or political relations; and so far inferior, that they had no rights which the white man was bound to respect; and that the negro might justly and lawfully be reduced to slavery for his benefit. He was bought and sold, and treated as an ordinary article of merchandise and traffic, whenever a profit could be made by it."[4]

The rise of the Abolitionist movement also led to another period when Whites tried to justify race through scientific means. Again, the White assertion was made that those of African descent were inferior people. To support this claim, U.S. scientists drew on the racial theories of European scientists, like Carolus Linnaeus and Johann Friedrich Blumenbach, citing their "scientific justifications." These eighteenth and nineteenth-century scientists categorized racial groups as Caucasoid, Mongoloid, Australoid, Negroid, and Indian. Those who were not Caucasoid were seen as biologically inferior and indeed subhuman. White scientists studied physical differences and conducted anatomical investigations to prove that other racial groups are inferior to the White race. Social Darwinism also became popular in America as a race science justifying the belief in White superiority. These beliefs were used to justify the extermination of Native Americans and the continued oppression and segregation of African Americans. Prominent educators promoted these ideas, like Samuel Cartwright, who wrote the article "Negro Freedom Impossibility under Nature's Law" (1861), and Frederick Hoffman, who wrote, "Race Traits and the Tendencies of the Negroes" (1896) that sought to provide a statistical way of describing Negroes as being inferior to Whites. John Fiske (1842–1901) at Harvard and William Graham Sumner (1840–1910) at Yale used Social Darwinism to justify the extermination of Native Americans. Madison Grant (1865–1937), as the chair of the New York Zoological Society and Trustee of the American Museum of National History, advocated segregation, sterilization, eugenics (selective breeding), and population control among the Negro population. Ian Hannaford, in his book *Race: The History of an Idea in the West*, provides a full elaboration of the thinking of Fiske, Sumner, and Grant. This formed the academic as well as cultural support for racial segregation and miscegenation laws. The racist ideology claimed that African Americans should be segregated from Whites so that they would not contaminate White society. The dominant view became clear—treating People of Color as equals to Whites would cause the deterioration of all that is noble, pure, and superior in the White race. These prominent educational viewpoints also contributed to the systemic racism that shaped life in America.

Fast forward to today and consider the push-back that has emerged recently in some White communities to the *New York Times*' 1619 Project and other academic efforts to narrate our nation's history of racism. In the past year, conservative lawmakers and politicians have made a concerted effort to limit the teaching of "critical race theory" in public education. Critical race theory is a historical framework developed more than forty years ago to provide an understanding of how racial disparities have developed and endured in America for centuries. The seminal idea within this historical perspective is that racism has been grounded in beliefs about White supremacy and this racial belief has been ingrained in the structures of our society to create economic, educational, and housing gaps between Whites and People of Color. Many conservative Whites, however, suggest that teaching the history of slavery and Jim Crow–era policies should only address the "facts" without their social implications. They claim this perspective is actually dangerous and implies that America is still a racist nation. The political move by Whites to prevent critical race theory from being taught is a current form of White denial about the impact of the racial values of our European ancestors have woven into the fabric of America. By ignoring or sanitizing this history of racism, White people today are kept from appreciating the difficult experiences and massive injustices that People of Color in this country have endured for generations.[5] This has led to what Bryan Stevenson, the founder of the Equal Justice Initiative, has called the "White empathy deficit" regarding the struggles against oppression that People of Color have faced and had to overcome in the history of our country. Without unpacking the long reach of systemic racism in our nation's history, as unpleasant and troubling as it may be for those of us who are White, we are not likely to confront the roots of our racial biases that reach into our lives today.

Finally, we should note when the subject of race comes up today, many of us like to take consolation in the belief that we have made significant progress over the past fifty years in erasing individual and systemic racism. At the same time, many Whites become impatient and even hostile when People of Color complain about unfair treatment by Whites and unrelenting racial injustices that they continue to experience. This has been particularly evident within segments of White America with respect to the Black Lives Matter movement. The White counterclaim that "all lives matter" is one example of the desire within the White community to minimize the prevalence of racial discrimination that still exists in this country. The problem with the White rejoinder "all lives matter" is not that it is untrue. Rather, the problem is with the quickness and the ease with which Whites turn to such universal formulations about our common humanity. Such well-intended gestures to universal humanity, using colorblind discourse, ignore not only the history of racism but also the legacy of White racial biases that still exist today. Colorblindness is assumed to stem from "good" intentions, yet such discursive moves allow one to "miss the fact that Black people have not yet been included in the idea of 'all lives.'" This claim that "all lives matter" just re-centers White interests and needs over the needs and concerns of People of Color.

Those of us who may wish to become part of the anti-racist movement today cannot be naïve about the challenges involved in undoing racism in America. White responses to the growing awareness in America about racial injustices and inequities impacting People of Color also reveal a troubling White cultural reassertion of White supremacy and privilege on the part of those of us who hold conservative, right-wing political viewpoints. This reassertion of cultural Whiteness was evident among the "insurrectionists" at the January 6, 2021 political rally in Washington, DC, who invaded our nation's Capitol Building to challenge the 2020 presidential election certification process. These White insurrectionists represent an element in our White society who feel marginalized and threatened by government actions that limit their personal freedoms and that contradict their nationalistic views about America. While often unspoken, many of these Whites reflect a personal sense of loss about today's cultural condemnation of White supremacy and White privilege. Therefore, we must not assume that all White people want to affirm and embrace the benefits of living in a multicultural and multiracial nation of diversity, equality, and freedom for all. If the history of the U.S. tells us anything, we should be prepared to address a power struggle among Whites about maintaining or giving up White privileges.

Without stopping to unpack how and why the complexity of systemic racism has shaped America to this day, most of us who are White will not be prepared to confront the roots of our embedded racial biases that may reside in us as individuals or within the structures of our nation's institutions.

CHAPTER FIVE
CONFRONTING AMERICA'S WHITENESS STANDARD

"Since the notion that we should all forsake attachment to race and/or cultural identity and be 'just humans' within the framework of White supremacy has usually meant that subordinate groups must surrender their identities, beliefs, values, and assimilate by adopting the values and beliefs of privileged-class Whites, rather than promoting racial harmony this thinking has created a fierce cultural protectionism."

—bell hooks, *Killing Rage: Ending Racism*

"Ultimately evil is done not so much by evil people, but by good people who do not know themselves and who do not probe deeply."

—Reinhold Niebuhr

So, in view of our nation's racist history, the question we must ask is why these racial distinctions have been so important to White-skinned people. The facts may be uncomfortable for Whites to admit, but they have to be faced. In some real sense, White racism was birthed out of the economic interests and benefits of Western Europeans who came to establish colonies on the North American continent. As I have noted about our U.S. history, the "White man" claimed the land that Native Americans inhabited to take the territories they had occupied for thousands of years without needing to pay anything. This White settler's land grab was repeated in lands owned by Mexico. We don't teach our children that this land theft by Western Europeans was based on the idea of White superiority, with claims that Native peoples were "savages," uncivilized, and heathens.

The racial biases about skin color are obvious in the terms that White pioneers used to identify those they wanted to evict from the land, calling the indigenous people "savages." By dehumanizing these non-Whites with non-European cultures, the Whites with European ancestry simply confiscated these lands through broken treaties, violence, genocide, and later with resettlement measures that isolated Native Americans on "Indian Reservations." In our White glorified history, White Europeans used military force, economic deals, legal means, and missionary zeal to push Native Americans and Mexicans off their land both before and after Africans were brought here in chains as slaves for cheap labor under the same White superiority belief system. Our White national legacy of racial discrimination based on beliefs about a superior skin color was initially tied to economic benefits for the earliest European colonizers.

Those of us who were indoctrinated in the 1950s and 1960s by TV shows about "cowboys and Indians" know full well that the White man was depicted as the good guys while the Indians were cast as the murderous savages. According to the White historical narrative of our nation, we seem to have forgotten about the ethnic cleansing of Native Americans that was justified in the name of moral, religious, and cultural progress. In fact, the social and political inclusion for White people and the exclusion of People of Color were written in the earliest governmental documents of this new nation. This can be seen in the very first naturalization law, enacted in 1790 to establish guidelines for how immigrants could become American citizens, which limited citizenship to "White" persons. For all the idealizing of the principles of freedom and equality that are contained in the foundational documents of the United States of America, the Constitution developed for our nation made it explicitly clear that only White men counted as full citizens deserving of such freedom and equality. The most horrific war that our nation has ever fought was over these inherent racial biases upon which this experiment in democracy was supposedly established.

Even as the U.S. has become more racially and ethnically diverse, this dominant White racial standard has stood in the background. The primary feature of this White cultural standard has been the belief that White-skinned people are inherently superior to darker-skinned people in a variety of ways. This age-old White-generated and White-sustained belief system is what I call *the ideology of White superiority*.

As I have said earlier, one of the most helpful explanations I have found regarding this perception about racial differences is contained in Joe Feagin's analysis of what he calls the "White racial frame."[1] At its core, the "White racial frame" uses light skin color as the basis for determining admirable human characteristics and the stereotyping of darker skin persons as less capable or admirable. For centuries now in the U.S., this dominant White identity has promoted racial prejudices and ideologies that elevate any and all White-skinned people, regardless of our behavior or talents, over dark-skinned people. As Feagin points out, this social preference toward White-skinned people is rooted in Western European intellectual traditions dating back at least to the eighteenth century. Under the guise of science, some of the earliest European biologists developed distinct classifications of humanity based on "racial" characteristics of skin color and facial features from so-called studies of African peoples. In short order, these biological classifications were combined with philosophical and theological ideas about a hierarchy of values, which was thought to characterize all of reality. So, to understand the ideology of White superiority, it is important to understand the intellectual foundation of this belief system that George Lipsitz has called a "pigment of imagination."

The primary belief that all reality and everything that exists reflects a structure of "greater" to "lesser" levels of value has been identified as the idea of a *Great Chain of Being*, as described in A. O. Lovejoy's book by that title. Sometimes called the *Scala Natura* (scale of nature), this ancient view of the world suggested that creation exists within a universal hierarchy that stretched from God (or immutable perfection) at its highest point down to the inanimate matter at its lowest. In the hands of philosophers and theologians, each level of existence in the Great Chain of Being represented a distinct category of living creatures or forms of matter. Those creatures or things higher on the chain possessed greater intellect, movement, enjoyment, and ability than those placed below. To this hierarchical way of thinking, each level of existence possessed all of the attributes of the level below plus an additional, superior attribute. In this hierarchy of beings, reasoning human beings are superior to animals, animals are superior to plants, and plants are superior in their life form to lifeless rocks and dirt. This presumed structure to life was given theological justification in the Middle Ages through the beliefs that God instituted this hierarchy of value, from the "superior" down to the "inferior." To this way of perceiving the world, God represents the highest level of value; angels were divine creatures above humans; humans, by virtue of conscience and intellectual acumen, were above animals; and animals were above unconscious beings like plants, rocks, and matter, with each declining level having less value. The biblical witness reflects this hierarchical way of thinking in its claim that humanity was created in the image of God and was given dominion over the animals, plants, and the rest of the created world. In this ancient conceptualization of life, there were sub-levels of value among humans. Females were seen as being inferior to males. The Hebrews, as God's chosen people, were superior to the pagans and infidels. Later on, Christians viewed themselves as being closer to God and superior in faith to other religious traditions. Greek and Roman civilizations were regarded as superior to other, less advanced civilizations. In time, Eurocentric beliefs about the primacy of their culture led conveniently to the view that God had created humanity into superior to inferior races, with White-skinned people being said to be superior in intellect, morality, motivation, and ability to dark-skinned people. By the eighteenth century, the European assigned values for the diversity within human life had become racialized so that White-skinned people were assumed on the basis of nature to be superior to dark-skinned people. In the hands of European and American scientists, a taxonomy of racial identities was developed, which characterized dark-skinned people, in sharp contrast to White people, as being bestial and apelike, unintelligent, uncivilized, immoral, rebellious and oversexed, lazy, and dangerous.

Sociologists like Feagin have argued that this culturally skewed European idea of superior and inferior races became the basis for what has been known as "White supremacy." This White racial frame has consisted of (a) the use of skin color and facial features to differentiate between social groups, (b) the linking of "racial" characteristics to positive and negative cultural distinctions, and (c) the belief that White people are somehow more culturally, intellectually, and morally superior to other racially defined groups of people. This racial framing has become a "comprehensive orienting structure" for Whites in America to interpret everyday experiences. As Feagin suggests, this European White racial framing justified the dehumanizing beliefs and practices that the earliest English-speaking settlers inflicted on both Native Americans and African slaves.[2]

The beliefs about White supremacy among the races, at least among most White-skinned people, has consistently shaped the racial and cultural interactions of White and Black folks in America from the days of slave trading of Africans in the seventeenth century, through the abolition of slavery in the nineteenth century, to the Jim Crow era into the twentieth century, and right up to today. The importance that White people in this country have put on darker skin colors as a racial barrier to social acceptance and to limit civic rights and privileges for People of Color is clearly evident in the "separate but equal" laws that arose out of the *Plessy v. Ferguson* Supreme Court decision of 1896, the use of the brown paper bag test, voter literacy requirements, anti-miscegenation laws, and a host of other ways that Whites devised to oppress, restrict, and marginalize People of Color often in the name of maintaining White racial purity.

The prominence of this White racial framing in American history now seems to be ignored or overlooked by our dominant White population. Maybe our historical blindness to the impact of racism on our nation can be attributed simply to the notion that the winners always get to write the histories. It shouldn't be surprising then that White people remember and tell "our country's history" in the most positive terms. There is also ample historical evidence to support the White attitude that People of Color have represented a four-hundred-year-old "problem" for our American (aka, White) way of life. The White need to confirm the belief in White superiority is clearly evident in the enslavement of Africans for cheap labor in the colonies before and after the formation of the United States of America. The importing and selling of African slaves were profitable businesses in the agrarian South. After the emancipation of the enslaved during the Civil War, unquestioned White supremacy remained firmly in place through the establishment of Jim Crow laws during the Reconstruction period, the passage of the Chinese Exclusion Act, and during the civil rights struggle in the 1950s and 1960s to end racial segregation in America.

When the Swedish minister of trade and commerce, Gunnar Myrdal, was invited to come to the U.S. in the 1940s to study "America's Negro problem," he candidly observed that the belief in White supremacy established in this country was "the White man's theory of color caste," declaring the Negro to be in every aspect inferior to Whites and, therefore, could not be assimilated into American society (see *An American Dilemma: The Negro Problem and Modern Democracy, Volumes One and Two*, 1944). Later, in response to the White fear that the racial riots of the mid-1960s generated, President Lyndon Johnson authorized in 1968 a commission to study the racial unrest going on in many U.S. cities. The Kerner Commission Report concluded that White racism and not Black anger had been the catalyst for the racial turmoil in America, brought about by abusive policing practices, a flawed justice system, poor or inadequate housing, bad lending practices, high unemployment, voter suppression, and other culturally embedded forms of racial discrimination that largely impacted People of Color. The assumption about White superiority continues even today, though it is often veiled. Remember, in the past four years, we have elected a president who equated White supremacy groups with the anti-racists wanting to remove Confederate monuments from their old places of honor.

Another dimension of the White racial frame shows up in the history of immigration in America. Historians, for instance, have noted the cultural assimilation struggles that Italians, Jews, Irish, and Middle Eastern ethnic groups faced during the late-nineteenth and early-twentieth centuries when they came to the U.S. seeking new freedoms and economic opportunities. While all these ethnic groups are commonly thought to be "White" or "Caucasian" today, there was a deep prejudice during this wave of European immigrants that they were not racially accepted as sharing the dominant White identity. This suggests that "Whiteness" has also been seen as a social-cultural trait signifying an inherent difference in humanity that goes beyond one's skin color.[3]

One of the characteristics of this White preferential orientation is the underlying desire of Whites to feel special, exceptional, and uniquely endowed within the human family. My reading of human history suggests to me that this desire to feel "special" or "exceptional" has existed throughout the ages and in every culture. Yet, this penchant toward thinking that "our" race, religion, national identity, gender, cultural values, or political ideology somehow makes us special or exceptional has led to most of the tragic wars and conflicts in human history. The history of racial discrimination in America has been predicated on the complexity of prejudices about White social purity and superiority regarding People of Color and some ethnic groups. Since the Emancipation Proclamation, African Americans have often gained social and cultural respectability only to the extent that "they" have appropriated White values and cultural standards. American history also suggests that this racially based Whiteness standard required People of Color to assimilate into the dominant White American culture and to take on White virtues in order to gain acceptance and have access the resources. This cultural preference toward those non-Whites who accommodate White virtues has sometimes been the source of tensions and conflicts between Latinos and African Americans vying with one another for economic and social acceptance by Whites.

Despite the growing awareness today about racial inequalities and injustices, little attention has been given to the dynamics of our White framing of racial identity and attitudes. So, I want to address two concepts or terms that are often used interchangeably to describe the root problems with our White racial framing. One of these involves the ideas about **White supremacy**, and the other is sometimes referred to as **White superiority**. While these terms are sometimes thought to be synonymous with one another, they often carry some different meanings for many of us. Elizabeth Martinez, in her paper, "What Is White Supremacy?", defines the first idea or concept in this way: "White Supremacy is a historically based, institutionally perpetuated system of exploitation and oppression of continents, nations, and peoples of color by White peoples and nations of the European continent, to maintain and defend a system of wealth, power, and privilege." This idea shares many aspects of what we also call the internalized ideology of racial superiority in that it too is comprised of "a complex multi-generational socialization process that teaches White people to believe, accept, and/or live out superior societal definitions of self and to fit into and live out superior social roles."

While White Supremacy is often a proper name given to White groups who claim White superiority among the races, the ideology of White superiority underlies many of the racial biases that many Whites still possess. In any case, these two terms reflect White attitudes and behaviors that normalize the race constructs long held by the dominant White culture in America.

To avoid making a shape or evasive distinctions between these terms, I am calling their shared construct the "Whiteness Standard." These ideas about White supremacy and White superiority have long inhabited our predominantly White Anglo-Saxon Protestant (WASP) country as the means to provide power and privilege to those who are identified as being White.

Many of us today only recognize beliefs about White superiority when this ideology is clearly articulated by overt White racists. Some of the clearer manifestations of the Whiteness Standard are still easiest to see in the Deep South, where slavery played a key role in the economic development of that region. In addition to the agricultural fortunes that were made on the backs of slave labor, the large number of slaves imported into the antebellum South also created widespread anxiety among White people about their safety and dominance over their Black slaves. White supremacy laws and social customs were developed to maintain control over these servile, Black-skinned people.

In "Notes on the State of Virginia," Thomas Jefferson stated his concerns about interracial sex for the new nation, claiming that Whites were "stained" when they mixed with Blacks, who he believed were inferior in mind and form (even though Jefferson himself has been linked to a sexual relationship with one of his slaves, Sally Hemming). Worries about maintaining White purity were codified into the miscegenation laws against interracial marriage up until the *Loving v. Virginia* ruling by the Supreme Court in 1967. Racist politicians like Strom Thurmond were re-elected to Congress in part because of their vocal views about White superiority and the need to maintain White racial purity.

Now that these overt forms of White superiority have faded away, many of us want to believe that the ideology itself has disappeared. I am arguing this is not the case. When conversations about race come up among Whites today, I hear too many comments about "us" and "them," suggesting that many of us continue to make broad racial distinctions and judgments. Even the Whites who can acknowledge the presence of structural racism in America sometimes complain that defining those of us with European ancestry by a toxic "Whiteness" doesn't lead to its cleansing. While this may be true for some, it is often the lack of awareness about how our "Whiteness" benefits us and disadvantages People of Color that perpetuates both systemic and structural racism.

In his important book *Racism Without Racists: Color-Blind Racism and the Persistence of Racial Inequality in America,* Eduardo Bonilla-Silva calls the racializing and socializing process that White people often exhibit our "White habitus." By this, he means a sense of belonging and solidarity with White people like us that also creates negative views about non-Whites. Moreover, Whites do not have to be reflective about our racial identity since "Whiteness" is considered to be the norm in America. From his sociological studies, Bonilla-Silva finds that "Whites do not see or interpret their own racial segregation and isolation (from People of Color) as a racial issue at all."

Consequently, our lack of awareness about how our White racial identity matters in our lives, along with limited interracial socialization, allow us to think that skin color is not really that important, at least not until we are put in a White-minority racial setting. For instance, my wife and I noted our own heightened sense of our White racial identity when we decided to attend an African American congregation where we were the only two Whites present.

Without deliberate efforts on the part of Whites to socialize with People of Color, we will remain trapped in our own racial frameworks and unable to appreciate how the ideology of White superiority and our White privileges manifest themselves among us. The structural and institutionalized benefits of Whiteness in America that are not evident to most of us show up most clearly in the inherited and accumulated wealth, educational opportunities, and access to health care that generations of Whites enjoy but are not in the experience of People of Color. The gain a better understanding of how this systemic investment in Whiteness functions, many of us should read George Lipsitz's book *The Possessive Investment in Whiteness: How White People Profit from Identity Politics.*

There is plenty of evidence as well that White claims about the natural and cultural superiority of "our race" and the inferiority of People of Color were not isolated in the Deep South to maintain the institution of slavery or to keep African Americans economically dependent. It is easy to lose sight of the policies that promoted White superiority in places in Oregon, which enacted in 1844 a "lash law" to be exercised against any Black person, slave or free, so they would be "whipped twice a year until he or she shall quit the territory." Later on, legislation was passed to keep Black people from coming to the state and barring them from residency right up to the twenty-first century. As a *New York Times* article stated in June 2017 in a report on the presence of White supremacists and hate groups in Oregon today, "While many Americans may think first of the South as the region where the burden of racial strife weighs heaviest on the nation's soul and psyche, recent events in Portland serve as a reminder that old battlefields are everywhere."

As recent history has shown, disrespect for the lives of People of Color has been disturbingly evident in cities in Northern states as in other parts of the country. The video of a police officer in Minneapolis putting his knee on the neck of George Floyd while this Black man was handcuffed on the ground, saying he was unable to breathe, reflected more than just a tragic example of police brutality and excessive force. It was difficult for the jury in the trial of the officer and for many White Americans not to see the officer's actions as devaluing of this Black man's life. The connection between an undeclared ideology of White superiority and the devaluing of the life of a Person of Color has been hauntingly evident in many such events in recent years.

My experience tells me that it is fairly natural for us as humans to notice visible differences between each of us as individual persons. Most of us learn early in life to see distinctiveness among people.

Preschool-age children are often embarrassingly quick to give voice to the differences they notice in people they encounter, particularly when they comment publicly about people with physical limitations, bodily scars or disfigurements, or some other trait. In a predominantly White society, it is not unusual for White children who have not been exposed to People of Color to notice what we call "racial differences."

White racial preferences have long been a part of the cultural landscape in America. Our Whiteness Standard shows up in the subtle but noticeable ways we use language to describe perceived realities. Listen, for example, to this litany of judgmental terms we associate with the colors "Black" and "White" penned by Jacqut James:

Blackmail, Blacklist, Black mark, Black Monday, Black mood, Black-hearted, Black plague, Black mass, Black market.
Good guys wear White hats, bad guys wear Black. We fear Black cats and the Dark Continent. But it's okay to tell a White lie, lily-White hands are coveted, it's great to be as pure as the driven snow. Angels and brides wear White. Devil's food cake is chocolate, angel's food cake is White! We shape language and we are shaped by it. In our culture, White is esteemed. It is heavenly, sun-like, pure, immaculate, innocent, and beautiful. At the same time, Black is evil, wicked, gloomy, depressing, angry, sullen. Ascribing negative and positive values to Black and White enhances the institutionalization of this culture's racism. (In the Storm So Long, 1991)

In my struggle with White racial biases, I have come to believe that James Baldwin's question about why Whites invented the idea of the "negro" contains the crux of the matter concerning the idea of White superiority. My experience with White racial biases has led me to think that there are at least three answers to his question:

1. The ideology of White superiority reflects the psychosocial need in many of us to be better than and to have more worth than someone else (self-esteem promotion at the expense of someone else). Sociologists like Barbara Ehrenreich and Gidron and Hall have described what they call "subjective social status" to indicate the value that individuals in America have placed on obtaining and maintaining respect within the social makeup of the country. This social respect is often defined by our beliefs about "where we stand relative to others in society." For many Americans who have not achieved social status via economic, educational, or political success, their White racial identity has often provided a manufactured level of respect within the larger social order.[4]

2. The ideology of White superiority represents the age-old human inclination toward tribalism and promoting an affinity toward "our kind," as opposed to those who do not share kinship or some other natural bond with us (a primitive human survival instinct often rooted in fear).

3. The ideology of White superiority embodies the human lust for power to control, dominate, and use others for our own selfish purposes. In his study of the history of racist ideas, Ibram Kendi came to understand that racism isn't rooted in ignorance and hate but in self-interest. Racist ideas, he suggests, have been created "to defend and rationalize the inequitable effects of (the) policies" that the powerful policymakers develop to serve their own self-interests, whether these are economic, social, political, or cultural benefits.[5]

As I said earlier, one of the defining characteristics of most forms of racism involves the use of power to establish and maintain discriminatory practices against People of Color. This is certainly the case for White people who have promoted and maintained ideas about the superiority of White skin color over dark skin. As the history of our nation demonstrates, White people have often provided a rationale to legitimize racial inequalities as a means for promoting shared racial self-interests. Without the dominant White community having the social, political, economic, and religious power to enact policies and to enforce them, the scourge of racism would not have manifested its ugly history and impact on People of Color in the way it has. So, the Whiteness Standard gains its negative, oppressive quality because our White society has had the power to impose our racial biases on others.

As many have observed, racism in America has often been framed as a problem for People of Color, rather than as a problem that White people have. Consequently, it is easy for Whites to talk about what People of Color can or should do to improve their lives and to escape racial biases. As long as we see the problems of racism residing with People of Color and not with those of us who are White, we will argue that "they" need to see the value of education, obeying the law, staying married to raise children, etc. Moreover, White people often want to treat the symptoms of racism that non-Whites suffer from rather than address the root causes within the White community. Instead of addressing our racial biases White progressives sometimes like to advocate for measures that benefit People of Color like Head Start programs, charity outreach to the poor, and reducing recidivism rates in the criminal justice system, etc. On the whole, most Whites today think we can eradicate racial injustices by giving People of Color more opportunities, or find ways to close the economic wealth gaps between the races, or to ensure that law enforcement and the criminal justice system treat People of Color more fairly. While these efforts are certainly needed, when Whites focus on these improvement strategies to fix People of Color, we rarely get around to addressing how our

White privileges and cultural beliefs provide us with advantages and acceptability that, in turn, create inequities between us and People of Color. In short, the "Whiteness standard" represents the values, experiences, and expectations by which we measure all racial identities and behavior. Dismantling this Whiteness Standard is the fundamental challenge I see us needing to address in order to achieve full racial equality and justice in America.

Oddly enough, this Whiteness Standard and its institutionalized racist expressions only became noticeable for many of us in America when it was evident in the South African practice of apartheid under the White minority who had controlled the nation's government and resources. This policy and practice of racial discrimination and segregation were instituted by the minority White, Dutch colonialists to maintain control over the predominately dark-skinned indigenous people of that country for generations. For some reason, it was easier for those of us in America to see institutional racism at work in the systemic government and social policies and economic and political structures embodied by the apartheid practices of South Africa than to see the same at work in our own country. At a distance, most of us who are White had very little difficulty understanding how the White Dutch minority, in this case, placed the majority racial groups at a disadvantage concerning their social, legal, and political rights and privileges. The bigotry within the White leadership of South Africa during the days of apartheid was apparent, and world sentiment for fairness and democratic principles caused a moral outcry against the White abuse of power. What is less apparent to many of us in the U.S. is how institutional racism often involves policies, practices, and behaviors that negatively impact minority People of Color in our country today. So, institutional racist policies in the U.S. have received far less public condemnation than the institutional racism of South Africa apartheid did. This appreciation for the impact that social, political, and economic policies have on the common good of a nation's citizens may explain why White people in Europe often see and lament the legacy of institutional racism here in the U.S. far more than most of us do.

Since the ideology of White superiority rarely makes it into our social studies textbooks or our educational exploration of racism, most Whites do not recognize or appreciate how we have been infected by this racial bias. When this pernicious racial ideology is pointed out, many Whites argue that we should not be held responsible for the racist sins and shortcomings of our ancestors. But this point of view fails to appreciate what has been called our national "identity," the stories we tell about our past that carry the values important to us. When we neglect to remember our nation's promotion of White superiority, we are adding to the myth that White people represent America at its best. Challenging the ideology of White superiority starts with acknowledging our White history of racial discrimination and confronting the overt and subtle ways that we have celebrated our White racial identity while marginalizing People of Color. As Ken Burns, the historian of public television education, has suggested, when we "forget the great stain of slavery that stands at the heart of our country, our history, our experiment," we forget who we are, and we make the rift between Black and White even greater. Penetrating the contemporary ideology of White superiority with all its masks and disclaimers takes a real effort to look closely at how People of Color have been labeled and treated in our nation's history as second-class citizens. The insidious and destructive aspects of these identifications of White superiority have shown up in some of the most brutal, violent, and inhumane ways imaginable in human relationships. White fear that their African male slaves would rape

White women if given a chance, and fear of losing control over their valuable human property reinforced moral sanctions against People of Color in the name of White purity. At the same time, White overlords found it somehow acceptable to fulfill their sexual desires with female slaves. Ironically, all of these sexual taboos and liberties were played out under White racial domination even as the slave masters tried to Christianize their slaves. Some of the most startling racist beliefs and sanctions can be found in the sermons being preached in Southern churches before and even after the Civil War. Many, if not most, Southern Christian leaders gave religious justification for the institution of slavery by claiming that God had created a superior race to rule over an inferior race. To this way of theologizing, it was the responsibility of White people to Christianize their heathen slaves and provide them with an opportunity for salvation in the name of Christ, at least to benefit them in the afterlife. The Bible was, therefore, interpreted to defend the institution of slavery and to spell out the divinely authorized relationship between masters and their slaves.

As one esteemed Presbyterian minister claimed in his 1861 sermon: "(God) has included slavery as an organizing element in that family order which lies at the very foundation of Church and State. A study of such words is, therefore, a first and an important step in ascertaining the will of God concerning an institution which short-sighted men have indiscriminately and violently denounced, and which wicked men have declared unworthy of the countenance of a Christianity whose peaceful and conservative spirit, as applied to society, they neither respect nor understand."[6]

This Christian preacher went on to tell his congregation that they should look forward to the day when their slaves "will all be what the Bible would make them; a race whose love for the Master above will spread through their rejoicing millions a measure of sanctification which will convert their services into the very first of home-blessings, and their piety into a missionary influence for saving the Black man everywhere from the ruin of perdition." The only warning given in this sermon was against masters inflicting unnecessarily severe punishment upon their slaves. The social acceptance of this kind of religious justification for both slavery and White supremacy is evident in the fact that a group of men in the congregation asked the pastor if they could print and circulate this sermon in the community.

Not only do the historical records make it clear that maintaining the institutions of slavery and White supremacy were the primary reasons the Confederate states left the Union, the Declarations of Secession by the Southern states highlighted how White supremacy had been cast in legal and religious terms: "All White men are and of right ought to be entitled to equal civil and political rights; that the servitude of the African race, as existing in these States, is mutually beneficial to both bond and free, and is abundantly authorized and justified by the experience of mankind, and the revealed will of the Almighty Creator, as recognized by all Christian nations; while the destruction of the existing relations between the two races, as advocated by our sectional enemies, would bring inevitable calamities upon both and desolation upon the fifteen slave-holding States."[7]

If we look carefully, we can find many examples of how these old ideas about racial superiority and inferiority continue to be perpetuated here in "the Land of the free and the home of the brave." The demonizing of People of Color by White politicians often appears to reinforce this idea that Whites are the better race.

As one commentator noted recently in *Killing Other White People*, "Contrary to Mr. Trump's notion that 80 percent of White people murdered in the U.S. are killed by African Americans, pesky FBI statistics indicate that more than 80 percent of murdered White

Americans are killed by other Whites." (Blacks accounted for less than 15 percent of White deaths in 2014 and a devastating 90 percent of Black deaths. Neither of those statistics is anything to celebrate, nor are they suggestive of the epidemic of Black-on-White violence that Trump and other fact-averse racialists continue to bleat and tweet about.)

This kind of twisted, race-based logic can be taken to the absurd, as one activist suggested in his observation about "walking on the moon." He points out that, to date, only twelve humans have walked on the moon, and they were all White guys. So, following this logic, shouldn't we ask why other races hate the moon so much? He says we all know the answer to this silly question. Our space program has, from its beginning, given preferential opportunities to Whites who have made up the pool of astronauts selected to travel to the moon, often with the assumption that the brightest and most talented aviators are chosen for such assignments. Following this kind of logic, we might also conclude that racial minorities don't like to fly airplanes and are rarely among the most talented or capable ice skaters. In actuality, the selection of astronauts in our nation's space program reflects little more than educational and career opportunities given to Whites that have not been afforded to People of Color.

As I have suggested, the "Whiteness Standard" is deeply embedded in the very structures of American life and our institutions. As the systemic manifestation of racism, beliefs about White superiority show up in the practices and policies of our economic and government institutions such as schools, banks, retailers, and courts of law, where racial disparities are very evident and noticeable. Most of us don't notice these systemic and institutional dimensions of the Whiteness Standard because we continue to think of racism in terms of individual beliefs and behavior that discriminate against People of Color. We may be quick to condemn overt racist or explicit beliefs and actions when these cause death, injury, destruction of property, the denial of services, or opportunity for People of Color. However, institutional racism is more subtle and difficult for many of us to see but no less destructive and even more far-reaching.

As Kendi points out, systemic and institutional racism inhabit governmental policies, business practices, and legal procedures in ways that have a disproportionately negative effect on the access to opportunities and the treatment of racial minorities. The experience of People of Color suggests that racial discrimination continues to occur in society even when individuals and institutions do not intend to make distinctions based on race. Without being either intentional or malicious, systemic racial biases still negatively impact People of Color to this day. In order to fully dismantle racism in America, most Whites will need to recognize and address these hidden aspects of the Whiteness Standard. Systemic and institutional racial biases are evident, for example, in studies revealing the higher number of People of Color who are stopped by police officers and the heavier sentencing given to African Americans in our criminal justice system. As Kwame Ture (aka Stokely Carmichael) and Charles Hamilton explained in their landmark book *Black Power: The Politics of Liberation*, "When White terrorists bombed a Black church and killed five Black children, that is an act of individual racism, widely deplored by most segments of the society. But [when] Black babies die each year because of the lack of proper food, shelter, and medical facilities, and thousands more are destroyed and maimed physically, emotionally, and intellectually because of conditions of poverty and discrimination in the Black community, that is the function of institutional racism."[8]

Systemic racial biases, when they take on institutional forms, are also difficult for Whites to appreciate because these biases often get intertwined with economic disparities and cultural differences. Let's take one example: the hugely disproportionate numbers of African Americans and Latinos in our nation's criminal justice system. Those of us who know how the criminal justice system works realize the benefits of having enough resources to hire good lawyers to defend us when we break the law. So, the inability of many People of Color to hire good legal counsel contributes to the racial disproportions in the criminal justice system. The Southern Poverty Law Center has demonstrated this reality time and again. The vulnerability of African Americans dealing with legal issues has been compounded by both economic limitations and cultural expectations about our legal system. Most of us recognize how accumulated wealth impacts our lives in terms of creating educational opportunities and social connections. As a 2011 Pew Research Center report noted, the median wealth of White households in America is 20 times that of Black households and 18 times that of Hispanic households. The economic recession during 2005–2009 only made this racial wealth gap worse. Similarly, educational opportunities, access to health care, and participation in the civic process are all heavily impacted by family economics and inherited wealth.

Let me provide another example of the effects of systemic racial biases and how African Americans are impacted by these issues when it comes to the safety of their children. White families rarely need to have "the talk" with their teenagers, as African Americans do, about how to act when encountering law enforcement personnel. We can assume that police officers do not engage in racial profiling or use excessive force when our family members are confronted with law enforcement officers. Unlike African Americans, White people do not generally complain about retailers asking us for proof of identification when using credit cards or feel we are under surveillance by clerks in stores when we shop. Without ever having a serious in-depth conversation with a person of color about their experiences with racial biases, many of us can remain either naive about or blind to the institutional forms of racism that racial minorities regularly encounter.

Even more hidden from most Whites because of the legacy of our nation's systemic racism is the value system embedded in a society that supports and allows for racial inequalities via public policies that favor some and neglect others. In some ways, the failure of many White people to grasp the effects of institutional racism or systemic is understandable. We simply don't experience or normally see racial biases at work because we are part of the dominant culture.

One of the manifestations of systemic racism that is particularly difficult for most Whites to recognize is what some now are calling **"White privilege."** Many Whites simply do not understand how our skin color alone provides us with many social, economic, and political benefits that non-Whites do not receive. As Linda Faye Williams has noted in her research on White privilege in America, when we focus only on the dynamics of those who are considered to be "disadvantaged," we fail to see the dynamics that give "advantages" to others. In terms of the development of our nation's social policies, "Whiteness becomes normalized and invisible, and relations of dominance are submerged. As a result, Whites develop such a powerful sense of entitlement that they do not question their ability to pass out the spoils of racial discrimination in banking practices, the criminal justice system, housing markets, media representation, educational arrangements, and social policies to succeeding generations."[9] In short, many Whites like to think that we have "earned" all our advantages without ever considering the historical and cultural advantages that our skin color has provided for us but not for non-Whites.

So, how can Whites who are isolated from People of Color develop a clearer understanding of our racial privileges? Many of us are simply not aware that we are granted certain advantages or social benefits that People of Color are often not afforded because of the differences in our racial histories and backgrounds. One real-life resource that helps to demonstrate the dynamics of "White privilege" is a video entitled "The $100 Race." This video presents a college class exercise where a group of students is lined up on a football field to race for a $100 bill that the instructor says will go to the winner. Before the race begins with everyone standing on the starting line, the instructor makes a series of statements and invites every racer to take two steps forward if any of the eight or so statements he makes applies to them. The statements include taking two steps forward if someone other than yourself is paying for your college education, not counting an athletic scholarship. Another instruction says you can take two steps forward if you have never had to work to help your family pay their bills or put food on the table. An invitation is given for the participants to take two steps forward if they have ever had a private tutor to help them with their studies in school or if they had both a mom and dad with a college education encouraging them. As these questions are asked, those who can affirm these statements as applicable to them quickly move ahead before the start of the race. After asking a series of these types of questions, the instructor then asks those who have moved ahead to turn around and look back at those who have hardly moved off the original starting line. Most of those who have not moved very far are students of Color. He tells the students that this is a demonstration of how White privilege works. He suggests that those who are White are given advantages and opportunities that they did not earn or deserve through any effort of their own, but that will likely help them to win the race for the $100 bill. This is a compelling illustration of how Whites receive unnoticed generational advantages based on collective White racial preferences and opportunities that have not been afforded to People of Color.

Part of the difficulty we have in recognizing the dynamics that come from this aspect of the Whiteness Standard is that we do not readily see how these advantages and benefits that come to those of us who have White skin. In her work on race and gender issues in the 1980s, Peggy McIntosh famously listed fifty "privileges" that accrue from being identified as a White person in America. She suggested that these social and cultural benefits are enjoyed by White people but rarely are extended to People of Color. These "privileges" range from the ability of Whites to shop without the threat of being followed by security personnel, to our lack of experience with racial profiling or harassment by police, to our option to act however you choose without being seen as emblematic of an entire racial group. She noted how "White privilege" functioned in social interactions but is masked and hidden by the structures and actions of White domination that make possible and sustain our White racial hegemony. Her confession was telling: "As a White person, I realized I had been taught about racism as something which puts others at a disadvantage but had been taught not to see one of its corollary aspects, White privilege which puts me at an advantage."[10]

Needless to say, many White Americans to this day have trouble believing that our White skin color provides any of us with some social, economic, or racial advantage. This denial in itself seems to prove her point. Many racial sensitivity training sessions today include specific exercises aimed at helping Whites to recognize how our skin color alone provides us with subtle but important advantages that People of Color do not have. Christina Cleveland, an African American social psychologist and author, has suggested that White privilege works subtly in social contexts like the wind does in foot races. Sharing a White racial identity provides a wind at our backs to aid us, while a dark skin identity acts as a headwind to impede People of Color in achieving equal outcomes for equal effort. I have included in the last chapter of this book an encouragement for White people to participate in a mixed racial group exercise that demonstrates how White privilege works in practical ways.

Given the close association of gender bias with racial bias within the notion of a hierarchy of superior to inferior, some of the most insightful racial studies have come from females who are more sensitized to the patterns of domination and marginalization shared by both racists and misogynists alike. Andrea Smith, for instance, has noted that White supremacy is constituted by a separate and distinct but still interrelated logic. She envisions three pillars within this "logic" of racism: one she labels Slavery/Capitalism, another she labels Genocide/Capitalism, and the last one she labels Orientalism/War. She tries to show how the same logic for one form of White supremacy supported and added the other two.[11]

All of these have impacted the People of Color for generations and created untold traumas in their lives. Sadly, most Whites have not paid much attention to the struggles that People of Color have tried to express. A diverse set of African American voices through the ages, from Frederick Douglas to W. E. B. DuBois, to James Baldwin, to Malcolm X to bell hooks, have maintained that the "Whiteness standard" lies at the heart of the problem of racism and damages the lives of People of Color. White people, however, have been very slow to recognize this racial dynamic. Only recently has the critical study of Whiteness emerged in the academic field, with a realization that racism will only be dismantled when Whiteness is seen as the problem that creates the color line problem that W. E. B. DuBois noted in 1903. As a Harvard-educated African American, DuBois was one of the first to suggest that White people are

CONFRONTING AMERICA'S WHITENESS STANDARD

rewarded for their support of a system that concentrates power and wealth in the hands of a few. He called this reward system the "psychological wages of Whiteness." While he did not use the terms "White privilege" or systemic racism, DuBois suggested that the idea of White superiority allowed Whites to think of themselves as better than Black folks, regardless of how poor they are, how many hours they have to work, how their labor makes someone else rich, or how much education they may have. "I might be poor, but at least I'm not a nigger" is how White identity helps shape a disfigured humanity of hierarchy and punishment in the service of power and wealth. If White people are to work for an end to racial injustice, then we must come to understand how the psychological wages of Whiteness have (mis)shaped our identity and (de)formed our consciousness. As DuBois suggested over a hundred years ago until White people confront their internalized ideology of racial superiority, the dynamics of racism will be reproduced unconsciously.[12]

Not surprisingly, many contemporary African American voices continue to provide a social commentary about this "Whiteness Standard." Tony Morrison suggests that racist White people have a "distorted psyche" because they don't understand that racial identities are socially and culturally constructed realities created and perpetuated by Whites for our benefit. The comedian Chris Rock tries to use humor to point out the absurdities of this racial bias. He is quick to say that no matter what Black people do, they will always be Black and judged by White standards. His videos "A Special Message for White People" and "A Special Message for Unarmed Black Men" provide revealing insights into the contradictions and ironies of this Whiteness standard. Sadly, some Whites fail to see the irony that Rock is seeking to point out about the double standards of White racial bias and think he is imparting words of wisdom for Black people to heed.

Those who write web articles for the *Colours of Resistance Archives* continue to link notions about White supremacy directly to racial difficulties today. From their perspective, "White identity has mutated and evolved over the years, but its core belief in being racially 'better,' of being above others is deeply intact. When White people complain that Mexicans are taking their jobs; when Whites complain that Asian Americans are taking over their country; when White people complain that Blacks are ruining their neighborhood—this concept of ownership, of entitlement, is all based on the notion that this is a White society that is supposed to benefit White people."[13] This demonizing and blaming other racial groups for the ills and problems we face in America is now endemic in the political ideology and policies of our former President Trump and in many of our state houses today. No wonder White racism in America now seems to be experiencing a rebirth.

While many of us have not noticed this, both sociologists and social activists today have come to recognize that White cultural norms permeate our White-dominated society. Yet, these norms appear to be taken for granted and are seen as value-neutral to the White social groups that benefit from them. So, White norms create the standards by which racial "difference" is constructed. Scholars in the field of what is called "Critical Whiteness Studies," like Barbara Applebaum, seek to make explicit how Whiteness is a determinant of social power and to demonstrate how Whiteness works through its invisibility. Again, Whiteness often goes unnoticed for those who benefit from it, but for those who don't, Whiteness is often blatantly and painfully ubiquitous. As Applebaum has pointed out, "Until White people develop an awareness that critically questions the frames of truth and conceptions of the 'good' through which they understand their social world, DuBois' insight will continue to ring true."

Other academics like Charles Mills suggest that the ideology of White supremacy is to race what patriarchy is to gender. Iris Marion Young adds that White supremacy, as a form of oppression, is to be understood as a structural concept that is reproduced by the everyday practices of a well-intentioned liberal society. The ideology of White racial superiority, therefore, presumes a conception of racism as a system of privilege that White people, often unwittingly, perpetuate in what seems to White people as common, unremarkable, and sometimes even seemingly "good" practices and in the implementation of what seems to be racially neutral policies. As bell hooks has emphasized, "When liberal Whites fail to understand how they can and/or do embody White supremacist values and beliefs, even though they may not embrace racism as prejudice or domination . . . they cannot recognize the ways their actions support and affirm the very structure of racist domination and oppression that they wish to see eradicated."[14]

To confront the Whiteness Standard, I believe we have to work deliberately to erase both the idea of White superiority from our minds and our institutions *and* to redress the White privileges accorded to us but not to People of Color in our everyday living. This will require us to identify how this Whiteness Standard is often hidden within many governmental, business, and educational practices that perpetuate racial inequalities. The racial disparities in wealth accumulation between White and Black people, for example, can be traced back to the Social Security Act of 1935 when agricultural and domestic workers, most of whom were Black or Brown, were excluded from this government program because key White southerners did not want governmental assistance to change the agrarian system from which most Whites benefited. Likewise, in the National Housing Act of 1939, the property appraisal system in our country tied property values and eligibility for government loans to race. As I have already pointed out, in the 1960s and 1970s, the U.S. banking system used a system of "redlining" minority neighborhoods as a way to avoid giving home loans that were considered to be at risk of defaulting. Similar institutional practices that promote or endorse some form of racial discrimination can be found in the unequal treatment of Whites and People of Color in our nation's health care delivery system, in public education, and the criminal justice system.

One of the obstacles we must address in overcoming White racial biases resides in our response to this question: When we benefit from the Whiteness Standard that was not of our own making and often not within our consciousness, are we still complicit in the perpetuation of a racist ideology? I am among those who have come to believe the answer to this question is yes. This may be the most demanding part of this racism recovery process that I am suggesting for White people. As I have discovered, recognizing the Whiteness Standard, owning responsibility for our participation in it, and committing ourselves to purge the ideology of White superiority and White privileges are the burdens that White people must accept to overcome the perversity of racism that has crippled America's ideals from its beginning. Acknowledging how the Whiteness Standard infects us personally and our institutions as well is essential to this racial bias recovery process. But even then, we face deeper ego challenges. Confessions of privilege, according to Levine-Rasky, serve as a "redemptive outlet" through which Whites can perceive themselves as "good Whites" in comparison to those "bad Whites" who do not acknowledge privilege. As "good Whites," we can disregard how our seemingly good practices may be contributing to the maintenance of systemic injustice. The assumption is "that confessing to the inner working of Whiteness in their lives would redeem them from their complicity with racism." Levine-Rasky contends that there is a danger that by acknowledging our privilege, Whites may assume that we have "arrived" and that we do not have to worry anymore about how we are implicated in perpetuating both the Whiteness standard and systemic racism.[15] This is another dimension of the difficulties we face when seeking to free ourselves from our Whiteness Standard.

In recent years I have had to confess to a jaundiced attitude about White people who believe that racism, racial discrimination, and White privilege are not solely our problems. Some Whites will reject any responsibility for systemic racism or benefitting from the Whiteness Standard by proclaiming our White innocence, pleading ignorance of the dynamics of unconscious racial biases, or simply affirming their commitment to racial equality ideals. Certainly, those of us who do not experience racism firsthand or who live within White communities will likely not recognize the existence of systemic racism or the benefits we receive from our cultural Whiteness Standard. Consequently, we can relieve ourselves of having to consider how we might be complicit in perpetuating a system that has little negative impact on our lives. Without ever asking People of Color about their experience with racism, Whites will continue to believe we can accurately determine the efficacy of White privilege or systemic racism. To my mind, this amounts to little more than one spouse claiming he or she is free of any relational bias and, consequently, can best adjudicate any problem that may arise in their marriage.

Another difficulty that most Whites have in recognizing the Whiteness Standard resides in the way many of us get socialized. On the whole, our socialization process occurs within our dominant racial group through family attitudes, cultural education, the media, and institutional practices that emphasize and continue to perpetuate a belief in a hierarchy of racial value. Again, our socialization is predicated on the notion that white-skinned people are somehow superior to dark-skinned people. To help us understand this contextual dimension of White supremacy, Derald W. Sue has described this process in more technical sociological terms: "the manifestation of ethnocentric monoculturalism." Sue enlarges this socialization frame to include several attitudes and beliefs that maintain the inherent superiority of one group over another, including race, cultural heritage, ethnicity, nationality, sexual identity, and even religious affiliation. He outlines five dynamics that come into play in this hierarchy of socialization: (a) self-pride from being a part of the dominant group; (b) the inferiority of other groups based on perceived differences; (c) the power of the dominant group to impose their standards on other groups; (d) institutional biases codified in a particular culture; and (e) the invisible veil of White privilege. The history of White superiority thinking in America reveals that all of these dynamics have shaped race relations in our country in one way or another.[16]

As I have attempted to explain, it is vital for us to understand that the Whiteness Standard has been adopted and embedded for generations in not only our social relationships but in the economic, legal, political, governmental, educational, and even religious institutions that shape so much of our lives in this country. **Institutional racism** is the term often used to describe this element of the Whiteness Standard. One of the long-standing assumptions within institutional racism has been the idea that People of Color in America should assimilate into White culture and adopt White ways of living in the world, even though White-controlled institutional policies and practices often impose significant disadvantages on BIPOC. Most of us who are White rarely see the racial advantages and disadvantages that lay within our nation's institutional policies and practices. It usually takes a Person of Color to call out these racial disadvantages that result in inequities of various forms.

Housing policies in American over the past sixty years reveal one of the best examples of this institutional racism based on the Whiteness Standard. When someone points out the ongoing amount of racially segregated neighborhoods in our cities or communities, some Whites claim that it is only natural for people with different skin colors to want to associate with those who look like themselves; in the same way, we gravitate toward those who share our economic status or political affinities. This "birds of a feather stick together" mentality shifts the issue away from racial biases to tribalism.

No doubt such tribalism comes into play with some of the effects of racism, but rarely is it the cause. There also seems to be, for many of us, an ego-need to claim some social status over others, particularly those who do not share our cultural or ethnic backgrounds, our intellectual and educational achievements, our religious viewpoints, our sexual or gender orientation, or our economic status. It is interesting to note that some conservative social commentators today, like David Brooks, suggest the fragmentation we see going on within America has more to do with the idea that individual rights and responsibilities matter more to a moral way of life than protecting the common good of all. Speaking about social issues, Brooks says, "The core problem today is not tribalism. It's excessive individualism, which has eaten away at our uniting faith and damaged our relationships with one another. Excessive individualism has left us distrustful and alone—naked Lockeans. When people are naked and alone, they revert to the tribe. Tribalism is the end product of excessive individualism."

What he doesn't say is that tribalism, in turn, tends to look for scapegoats and others not like us to blame for the social failures we see around us. The history of racism in America certainly seems to support the reality of a White tribalism dynamic, at least in what Carol Anderson has called "White Rage." She outlines how every time African Americans make some progress in overcoming structural racism, there has been some counter-effort in the White community to dismantle or negate that progress. As Anderson says, "This is the moment now when all of us—Black, White, Latino, Native American, Asian-American—must step out of the shadow of White rage, deny its power, understand its unseemly goals, and refuse to be seduced by buzzwords, dog whistles, and sophistry. This is when we choose a different future."[17]

Finding ways to rid ourselves of these various facets of the Whiteness Standard we may have inherited is indeed essential to overcoming racism and imagining a future of freedom, equality, and justice for all of us. As I have suggested, one piece of this effort involves the rejection of hierarchical thinking, which imagines people as having levels of intrinsic value according to skin colors. Abandoning this hierarchical thinking and tendency to categorize human traits and identities along a continuum of superior to inferior—in which males have more value than females, the intelligent and the strong ought to rule the mundane and the weak, royalty deserves respect and obedience of the masses, the religious are better than the heathens, etc.—will be a huge psychological, intellectual, and social challenge for people all around the world. I would argue that this kind of hierarchical thinking has been the source of some of the most destructive behavior in human history. Today we know that the differences in skin colors are the result of how much melanin that individuals genetically produce, principally from an ancestral history of exposure to higher levels of sunlight that contribute to darker skin tones. Likewise, human genome studies indicate there that the old racial distinctions within humanity are extremely exaggerated, and all people are part of one human race. Science, education, and interfaith religion can all help eliminate these ancient notions about "natural" differences and the inherent value of certain human beings. Another equally important piece of this effort resides in our psychological capacity to affirm the intrinsic individual worth of every person and to affirm the social belonging of everyone without needing to compete with others or emphasize our differences.

In conclusion, the racism recovery process I am proposing involves a conscious effort to replace the Whiteness Standard and its hierarchical racial thinking about people in terms of who is better than whom with the idea that there is only one human race. Liberating ourselves from the ideology of White superiority and the benefits of White privilege is a demanding exercise because we will be asked to give up the power that White identity has bestowed on us. Affirming our common humanity in all its diversity is critical to eradicating the Whiteness Standard that has shaped so much of America for generations. Such a conscious effort presents three challenges for those of us who are White: (1) to recognize whatever elements of the Whiteness Standard that may be embedded in us and to work at removing those biases; (2) to identify and remove the advantages, privileges, and concessions our White culture has historically made for Whites within our institutions and public policies; and (3) to embrace the opportunities and benefits of living in a culturally diverse nation with people of many racial identities and ancestries. I will now turn to how we might go about addressing these challenges.

CHAPTER SIX
ACCEPTING THE WHITE BURDEN TO ERADICATE RACISM

While I do want to underscore that I embrace color-blindness as a legitimate hope for the future, I worry that we tend to enshrine the notion with a kind of utopianism whose naiveté will ensure its elusiveness. In the material world ranging from playgrounds to politics, our ideals perhaps need more thoughtful, albeit more complicated, guardianship. By this I mean something more than the "I think therefore it is" school of idealism. "I don't think about color, therefore your problems don't exist." If only it were that easy.

—Patricia Williams,
Seeing a Color-blind Future: The Paradox of Race

As I have stated, the path toward eradicating racism in American resides with Whites accepting our responsibility for overcoming the racial biases that continue to perpetuate racial inequities and injustices in our nation. The process I have proposed for White people to do this involves confronting and eradicating, both individually and collectively, whatever White racial biases we may have inherited and the privileges given to us on the basis of our White identity. I stand by these convictions for several reasons. First of all, the White community has benefited for generations from the ideology of White superiority, and only our White community can reverse and purge this mindset.

As African Americans like Ibram Kendi have argued, the expectation that People of Color should assimilate White culture is in itself a racist idea founded on the old notion that White culture is somehow superior to cultures of People of Color. The problems we continue to have with race in America rest almost exclusively on White attitudes, perceptions, privileges, and long-held beliefs that our light skin color alone somehow makes us a better class or type of people. White identity affirmations exist primarily in the minds of White people for self-serving purposes. Science has now discovered that the categorizing of humanity according to "races" developed by Whites has no basis in genetics or biology. However, it has long been in the social, economic, and political self-interests of White people to keep this classification of people by skin color and ancestral heritage in place for hundreds of years. As White people, we must let go of this fallacy in the same way previous generations had to let go of the idea that the world is flat or women shouldn't be allowed to vote.

Confronting our White racial myopia is a big part of this challenge. As I have maintained from my experience addressing racial issues, White people can be so invested in our own cultural ways of thinking and acting that we often cannot see how our racial biases impact non-Whites. This is why I emphasize that we need People of Color to help us in our efforts to free ourselves from the burden of our racial biases that we do not easily recognize. But how are People of Color to help us with "our problem" when so many White people either deny, avoid, or become defensive about our racial prejudices? It seems to me that the onus of responsibility for dismantling racism and initiating courageous conversations about race begins with Whites who can humbly accept that we may need to reprogram our hearts and minds with regard to the virtues of our White identity. This is not an easy task. Many of us are so invested in our White belief systems and cultural values that it is hard for us to ask for help uncovering our racial biases, particularly without engaging in micro-aggressions toward People of Color. About the best we can do is to let People of Color know that we as Whites have serious issues with our racial biases and to graciously invite them to help us become more aware of how our White privileges and White biases show up in their experience with us and in our attitudes toward them.

Humility, openness to criticism, and respectful honesty are key to this kind of engagement with People of Color. Sociological studies indicate that when Whites recognize racial identities rather than claiming "colorblindness," we begin to develop empathy toward the experiences of others not like us. Moreover, as those of us who are White come to understand ourselves as members of a dominant racial group that enjoys unearned privileges and benefits, we are more apt to embrace a White identity built on antiracism rather than simply maintaining White cultural values.

Resisting our White defensiveness and avoiding pleas of ignorance and innocence about racial issues will be important in building trust and engaging in honest conversations with People of Color. Listening carefully and with the desire to learn what we don't know or understand is vital, especially when it comes to systemic and institutional aspects of White racial biases we rarely see. Once we have a better awareness of how People of Color are impacted by White racial biases, we then must work on liberating ourselves and other Whites from the racial biases and privileges we discover we have. I believe this was the point that Malcolm X, the radical Black power champion of the 1960s, was making when he said in his autobiography:

I have these very deep feelings that White people who want to join Black organizations are just taking the escapist way to salve their consciences. By visibly hovering near us, they are "proving" that they are "with us." But the hard truth is this isn't helping to solve America's racist problem. The Negroes aren't the racists. Where the really sincere White people have got to do their "proving" of themselves is not among the Black victims, but out on the battle lines of where America's racism really is—and that's in their own home communities; America's racism is among their own fellow Whites. That's where sincere Whites who really mean to accomplish something have got to work.[1]

So, as those who most often control the power structures in this country, White people need to find the courage to do their soul-searching to recognize our embedded racial biases that inhabit us as individuals and in the nation's institutions. A good place to start this exploration into embedded racial biases is actually with other Whites in order for us to avoid being anxious about what we might say to People of Color. Whether we engage in race conversations with other Whites or with People of Color, we have to initiate these conversations and accept that we might hear feedback that makes us very uncomfortable or even angry.

It is also important for us to understand that asking People of Color to share with us their experiences with White racial biases places a psychological and social burden on them as well. After years of White people using our skin color as a badge of superiority, building trust across racial lines will take time and effort on our part. Like any trusting relationship, establishing a friendship has to occur before any of us are likely to express emotional vulnerability and tell someone how we have been hurt.

I have learned that broken relationships of any type have the best chance for healing when one or both parties can find the emotional strength to initiate a conversation aimed at reconciliation *and* are willing to admit their part in the relational brokenness. So, likewise, Whites must be committed to participating in open, honest, and emotionally vulnerable conversations with both Whites like us and People of Color before we can expect any significant healing to occur.

As I have noted earlier, White empathy for the victims of racism and racial discrimination is essential in this process. As a White Christian who is seeking to come to terms with his own racial recovery, Daniel Hill appreciates James Baldwin's statement that "to be Black in this country and to be relatively conscious is to be in a state of rage almost all the time." Hill suggests that to be White in America and relatively conscious of the benefits of our Whiteness should leave us in a state of lament almost all the time.[2] Sadly, most White people are neither conscious of the benefits of our Whiteness nor lamenting the harm that the ideology of White superiority has done for centuries now to People of Color.

All of us who are White should keep in mind that engaging in conversations about race is often more difficult for People of Color than for us. Listen to what one Black person had to say to a congregation about why he avoids conversations with White people about race:

Living every single day with institutionalized racism and then having to argue its very existence, is tiring, and saddening, and angering. Yet if we express any emotion while talking about it, we're tone policed, told we're being angry. In fact, a key element in any racial argument in America is the Angry Black person, and racial discussions shut down when that person speaks. The Angry Black person invalidates any arguments about racism because they are "just being overly sensitive," or "too emotional," or playing the race card. Or even worse, we're told that we are being racist (Does any intelligent person actually believe a systematically oppressed demographic has the ability to oppress those in power?). But here is the irony, here's the thing that all the angry Black people know, and no calmly debating White people want to admit: The entire discussion of race in America centers around the protection of White feelings.[3]

This distrusting Black man is reluctant to have a conversation about race with a White person because of the differences in which we frame racism. "Black people, thinking as a group, are talking about living in a racist system. White people, thinking as individuals, refuse to talk about 'I, racist' and instead protect their own individual and personal goodness. In doing so, they reject the existence of racism."[4]

When we listen to some of the leading intellectual voices within the African American community, we can also hear a clear recognition that Black folks have some racial liberation and reconciliation work to do on their own. Cornell West, for example, has argued in *Race Matters* that Black folk suffer from what he calls "nihilistic despair"—a sense of unworthiness and depression due to generational living under the propaganda of White supremacy. This reflects the social and psychological damage done to many Blacks by years of White racism. Consequently, some African Americans today have given up on the democratic ideal that America is a nation committed to freedom, equality, and the rights of every person. In some respects, African Americans must continue to find ways to embrace the kind of self-esteem and self-differentiation expressed in the Black power movement where "Black is beautiful," and White people do not set the social or cultural agenda for Blacks. The same can be said for those of Latino, Asian, and

Indigenous American descent.

Shifting our responsibility for undoing our White racial biases over to People of Color is another way we sometimes fail to accept the burden for eradicating racism. Whether intended or not, focusing on what People of Color can or should do to eliminate racism amounts to the psychological protectionism of White identity. Those who have explored the phenomenology of racial identities have concluded that race permeates multiple levels of lived experiences. They argue that some of our racial identity is a learned cognitive construct while a great deal of our racial identities are subconscious and pre-reflective attitudes transmitted to us through historical narratives about social status and cultural inclusion.[5]

Consequently, these psychological dimensions of social identity based on racial distinctions are more difficult to address and alter. For instance, coming to terms with our Whiteness amid the rapidly changing racial makeup in America can produce identity problems for the once-dominant White community. As Linda Alcoff has observed, those who "feel White" can experience identity disorientation and lose a sense of connection to community and history when they disassociate from White racism and repudiate their White privilege. She concludes, therefore, that:

Rational arguments against racism will not be sufficient to make a progressive move. As Whites lose their psychic social status, and as processes of positive identity construction are derailed, intense anxiety, hysteria, shame and resulting forms of projection and displacement are occurring. The most likely solution to this will be, of course, for new processes to develop that simply shift targets to create new categories of the abject through which to inflate collective self-esteem. This is already happening in revivals of nativism, the vilification of illegal immigrants, a state-sponsored homophobia, and so on. In other words, if it can no longer be maintained that Whites, collectively, are better than non-Whites, just by virtue of race, then by removing race as a standard, our social identity can be reorganized on the basis of citizenship, patriotism, shared values, religious practices, or other features that most Whites can believe they share with others.[6]

When those of us who are White discuss racism, recognizing this is primarily a White problem, we should expect that our conversations will be loaded with both emotional issues and rational explanations, particularly about our culpability. As I have said before, those of us who are sincerely motivated to address our own racist attitudes and our unconscious biases should recognize that we are not the best people to determine how racism resides in us or to what extent we have overcome our inherited racism. People of Color will determine the racial progress our nation is making and the degree to which we have overcome White superiority issues and removed our White privileges. So, being grateful for receiving open and honest feedback from People of Color about our White racist attitudes and behaviors is important to state up front when we engage in conversations about race.

Even when we might be ready to have a conversation with BIPOC about racial issues, finding opportunities to listen to their experiences and to hear their assessments of White racial biases is in itself difficult for most White people simply because of the racially segregated lives we continue to live in America. Most Whites will have to make a conscious effort to develop relationships with People of Color for dialogue on race issues to occur. Some faith communities can provide a bridge for developing interracial conversations if they choose to do so. In some communities, you can find a contingency of White congregations who are willing to join in solidarity with BIPOC congregations to address racial equality and justice issues. However, as a minister, it has been discouraging to me to discover that only a few predominately White Christian churches today want to engage in community efforts to talk honestly about race. Since Christian churches in America have historically played a role in justifying racial hierarchies, I believe White churches have a special responsibility to dismantle racism today. I recommend any Christian church that finds the courage to discuss racial issues from a religious perspective to consider a congregational read and discussion of Robert P. Jones' book *White Too Long: The Legacy of White Supremacy in American Christianity* (2020, Simon & Schuster). This may be too challenging for many churches to undertake given that Southern Baptist seminary presidents have recently pushed back on the insights of critical race theory that links White racial biases to economic, political, and religious beliefs and practices. Nevertheless, I believe racial reconciliation ought to be a high priority for every religious institution in America.

By now, we shouldn't be surprised when some Whites have great difficulty facing the legacy of White racism in America and acknowledging our nation's moral failures in living up to our democratic, religious, and social ideals when it comes to racial issues. The innate White desire to protect our character and to affirm American exceptionalism runs deep among many of us. As I have pointed out, the resistance to owning the racist history in America is particularly acute in the South, even today when the history of the Civil War, the Reconstruction era, and the Jim Crow era are discussed. It seems that Southern White pride makes it hard for those who had ancestors fighting for the Confederacy to own the fact that their family supported the institution of slavery or White supremacy, even though most of the secession documents developed by the Confederate states plainly state these reasons for leaving the Union.

My encounters with other southerners who have ancestors that fought for the Confederacy have led me to think that many of us desire to sanitize this racist history for the sake of family pride. Some of us go so far as to claim that most Confederate soldiers did not own plantations and did not directly benefit from slavery. In an attempt to exonerate our White ancestors from the immoral enslavement of African Americans, some suggest that few of those who fought on behalf of the Confederacy owned slaves. However, the 1860 U.S. census reveals that among the states that would leave the Union, an average of more than 32 percent of the White families owned enslaved people. Some states had far more slave owners (46 percent of families in South Carolina, 49 percent in Mississippi) while only a few states had less (20 percent of families in Arkansas).[7]

Moreover, many defenders of Southern heritage overlook the stated reasons about defending slavery and White superiority that the Confederate states gave for leaving the Union. The same desire to disconnect the historical truth about the explicit White supremacy symbolized in the erection of Confederate monuments in the South during the Jim Crow era can be seen among the arguments that these monuments were only intended to honor faithful soldiers. Many of us overlook or ignore the deliberate attempts by the United Daughters of Confederate Veterans to promote the mythology that the enslaved were treated well by their White masters and enjoyed a good life under bondage.[8] Preserving the virtues of White heritage is often far more important to many Whites than acknowledging the truth about our ancestor's allegiance to both the institution of slavery and the ideology of White superiority.

In the spirit of confessing the moral failures of the past, I believe the civic and religious leaders of our nation today could help with this acknowledgment and healing process by issuing a National Confession of the Sins of Racism—an apology for the oppression, inhumanity, violence, and injustices inflicted upon Native Americans whose lands were stolen and ancestors were murdered. Likewise, such a national confession must acknowledge the oppression, inhumanity, brutality and violence, and injustices inflicted upon Africans brought here in chains as slaves to provide the labor to create agricultural prosperity during the seventeenth and eighteenth centuries and whose descendants have been subjected to the same mistreatment for two more centuries. Moreover, this national confession needs to be extended to Latinos and Asians who also have been inflicted with oppression, inhumanity, and injustices from our nation's rapacious desire to extend our borders and to secure cheap labor for our prosperity.

To move beyond the horrors of White supremacy and oppression, I believe it is important for our nation today to ask forgiveness from People of Color for all of the examples of inhumanity and injustices that were done in the past, largely by our dominant White population. I am among those who argue that remembering and confessing the evil acts of our nation's racist past and asking for forgiveness in some tangible ways are necessary steps in the process of racial reconciliation for America. While we cannot undo the horrors, atrocities, and mistakes our White ancestors committed against People of Color, we must recognize that our nation has benefited economically, socially, and culturally from the suffering and mistreatment of non-Whites in our history. I will say more about how we might go about this national reckoning in the next chapters.

I am also among those today who believe our government needs to have a serious conversation about paying reparations for the injustices committed against Native Americans and African Americans in particular but not exclusively for past racial injustices. Yes, there are practical difficulties involved in determining the financial and lineage issues for such reparations. Nevertheless, I believe the conversation about reparations needs to occur at a national level for Whites in this country to take some moral responsibility for the harm that has been done to BIPOC families for generations.

It is sad to note that Congressman John Conyers and the Congressional Black Caucus found little support within Congress for years to even discuss or debate their legislative proposal calling for a formal apology for racial and economic discrimination against African Americans. There has been little interest among our nation's civic or religious leaders in the formation of a commission to explore the reparations issue and to find creative and redemptive ways to express these reparations. To say that White Americans today have "no culpability for past crimes and injustices" reflects in itself a White racial frame that wants to exonerate White people for any responsibility for the lingering effects of racism in America.

It is easy for us as White people to say that the genocide of Native Americans or the enslavement of Africans brought in chains to the U.S. are horrible events in our nation's past that ought to be relegated to a lamented history. This kind of distancing from the suffering and abuse of those whose cultural heritage was suppressed by genocide, violence, or slavery represents, I believe, a collective lack of White empathy about the history of racism in this country and a roadblock to racial reconciliation.

Perhaps the biggest challenge we face in accepting the White burden for undoing racial injustices and confronting our White racial biases resides in the loss of power and pride that many Whites feel when we are asked to let go of a belief we have firmly held about our identity. We should remember and acknowledge the difficulties that many Whites had during the civil rights era of the 1960s and 1970s when Whites were challenged about racial injustices and inequities. Let's not forget the angry mobs and the institutional maneuvers of those who were determined to defend White power and privileges against legislative efforts to end racial discrimination with institutional changes like school integration and the Equal Employment Opportunities Act to end employment discrimination.

The 2019 movie *The Best of Enemies* captured the real-life story of the racial struggle in Durham, North Carolina, to come to terms with the loss of White social and political power and privilege when the ideology of White superiority was challenged. This same struggle among Whites today to relinquish oppressive social, economic, and political power and privilege can be seen in the perspective offered by conservative commentators like Christopher Caldwell in his book *The Age of Entitlement: America Since the Sixties*.

Here is what Jonathan Rauch said in his *New York Times* review of this book's social analysis: "In Caldwell's telling, the Civil Rights Act, which banned many forms of discrimination, was a swindle. Billed as a one-time correction that would end segregation and consign race consciousness to the past, it started an endless and escalating campaign of race-conscious social engineering. Imperialistically, civil rights expanded to include 'People of Color' and immigrants and gays and, in short, anyone who was not native-born, White and straight—all in service of the task that civil rights laws were meant to carry out—the top-down management of various ethnic, regional and social groups."[9]

Such negative viewpoints reflect the White racial bias that all socially or politically generated racial equality measures harm freedom, equality, or the rights of White people. This resurgence of White racial biases can be seen in the recent court rulings about removing the "preclearance" requirements that were effective anti-racist measures in the 1966 Voting Rights Act. To remove the voting barriers that African Americans and Latinos in the South had experienced up to that time, this act gave the federal government oversight into state election practices in order to end discriminatory practices. The impact of the act quickly became obvious when voter participation among minorities increased dramatically in many Southern states, and numerous People of Color were elected to serve in both state and federal government.

In 2013, however, the district attorney for Shelby County, Alabama, filed a lawsuit against this preclearance oversight provision in the federal law, claiming that "times had now changed" since the Voting Rights Act was put in place and this requirement was no longer needed. This mostly White notion that racial discrimination practices no longer existed in state elections was advanced all the way to the Supreme Court. In the court's 2018 ruling, this preclearance provision was overturned, thus allowing states to once again pass voting requirements that unfairly target minorities. This was done in the name of protecting elections from voter fraud, even though there was little evidence that such fraud was taking place. Here in 2021, a number of Republican-led state legislatures have passed laws to limit or suppress voting opportunities that greatly marginalize BIPOC voters. It seems to me that this is just another example of how White privilege and power seek to discriminate against People of Color while sanitizing White racial biases in the name of protecting election integrity.

Another example of the resistance of many Whites to accept the burden for dismantling institutional racism can be found in the White responses to recent community demands to "defund police departments." This movement wants to shift resources away from repeated armed confrontations between law enforcement personnel and People of Color in order to create more non-fatal means to address public safety issues. Former President Obama commented recently on the negative reaction that many White people in America have to the idea of "defunding police" by observing the political difficulties inherent in this racial justice slogan, noting that it "unearths or excavates or escalates fears within the White population that somehow the African American community is going to get out of control in some way or is not respecting authority."[10]

The resurgence of overt White racism then showed up in the mob of Trump supporters who assaulted the Capitol Building on January 6, 2021, effectively dispelling the idea that all Whites support law and order when we feel our political viewpoints or fear-based biases are not recognized. In the minds of many Whites and former President Trump, supporters of peaceful Black Lives Matter protests somehow posed more of a threat to law and order in America than the insurrectionists who stormed the Capitol Building.

Most recently, the institutional forms of White racial discrimination arose when the Trustees at the University of North Carolina in Chapel Hill initially denied academic tenure to Nikole Hannah-Jones, an award-winning journalist who won the Pulitzer Prize for her "1619 Project" for the *New York Times*, when she was invited to join the faculty there. While Hannah-Jones' tenure appointment had been authorized by the journalism department and the university's dean and provost, concerns about her work on the *1619 Project* apparently expressed by a donor to the school of journalism led to the denial of a tenured position. After an outcry of discrimination by faculty, alumni, and students, the trustees of the university then voted to offer Hannah-Jones the tenured appointment, which she declined, instead to accept a position at Howard University where contributions of Black scholars would be more appreciated.

Finally, accepting the burden for undoing racism confronts us with the thorny question about how we can best go about dismantling our racial biases and the benefits of White privileges. This question draws us into a complex of White ego issues, including White cultural notions about demonstrating perfectionism, being "right" or well-informed, having good intentions and possessing moral virtues, taking the initiative and offering solutions to problems, and being accustomed to taking the lead in social contexts or having a right to be listened to and respected.

The examples of desire to control conversations about racism can be seen in two contrasting attitudes among Whites—those who are uncomfortable with the idea that we operate out of a White superiority culture and those who feel compelled to demonstrate our racial enlightenment. Both of these extremes reflect the assumed prerogative for us to decide how our Whiteness figures into racial issues today. It is fairly easy to see this White power dynamic embodied among those who want to deny that White racial biases even exist or that skin colors no longer matter that much in America today. Even some self-righteous "woke" Whites who want to stand with People of Color may use their solidarity to avoid confronting their own racial bias blindspots.

In recent years, there have been several research projects which focus on White identity development and learning how White people can become anti-racists. These efforts at dismantling racism and moving Whites out of our racial biases suggest that becoming an anti-racist is a developmental process for most of us. The developmental models describe stages or levels that White people need to move through in order to become anti-racists. One model presents a ladder of steps beginning with a) claiming and valuing White identity as being important to one's self-esteem, b) moving to claims that race doesn't matter, c) moving to defensiveness about having White privileges or power, d) then moving to a feeling of shame or guilt about one's Whiteness, e) moving on to an acknowledgment of one's White racial biases and privileges, f) and finally moving on up to taking responsibility for dismantling inherited racism and actively participating in both individual and collective action to establish racial equality.

Similarly, another antiracism model describes five stages of development, 1) beginning with Whites who have little or no contact with People of Color and little awareness of or interest in racial issues, to 2) those who defend White identities, superiority, and blame victims of racism, to 3) those who have some transformational experience that recognizes race matters, to 4) those who are willing to explore racial self-awareness and White privileges, to 5) those who are engaged in overcoming and redressing racism and working on cultural competencies.

As Sandra Lawrence and Beverly Tatum note, "For Whites, the process involves becoming aware of one's 'Whiteness,' accepting this aspect of one's identity as socially meaningful and personally salient, and ultimately internalizing a realistically positive view of Whiteness which is not based on assumed superiority." The suggestion here is for Whites to identify where we currently are on this racial bias continuum in order for us to seriously engage in a White racial recovery process.[11]

As I have tried to demonstrate in my own confession and in this work, we must recognize how difficult this critical awareness of our Whiteness and its privileges are for us. Several generations ago, the theologian and social critic Reinhold Niebuhr captured

CONFESSIONS OF A RECOVERING RACIST

this difficulty very succinctly:

> *The moral attitudes of dominant and privileged groups are characterized by universal self-deception and hypocrisy. The unconscious and conscious identification of their special interests with general interests and universal values, which we have noted in analyzing national attitudes, is equally obvious in the attitude of classes. The reason why privileged classes are more hypocritical than underprivileged ones is that special privilege can be defended in terms of the rational ideal of equal justice only, by proving that it contributes something to the good of the whole. Since inequalities of privilege are greater than could possibly be defended rationally, the intelligence of privileged groups is usually applied to the task of inventing specious proofs for the theory that universal values spring from, and that general interests are served by, the special privileges which they hold.*

> —From *Moral Man and Immoral Society: A Study in Ethics and Politics*

Dismantling racism in America continues to be a challenge today due to a constellation of factors, including the allegiance to the ideology of White superiority by some, White denial by others, the racial isolation of many Whites, our inability to see systemic racial biases, and an unwillingness to recognize and address racial biases in our nation's institutions. We might be encouraged by survey studies that consistently reveal that the old supremacist beliefs of the past are less openly acceptable to White majority groups in virtually all Western liberal democracies. However, these same studies indicate that more subtle and covert variants of racism (nationalism, xenophobia, claims about welfare dependence and lack of values on the part of racial minorities, etc.) have emerged to justify negative attitudes by Whites toward People of Color. Many social psychologists suggest that White racial biases have now gone underground, and they have gathered substantial evidence that these biases thrive in subtle forms not as easy to recognize as in the past. According to one set of researchers, "The empirical evidence suggests that measuring racism only as overt individual bias may systematically understate the ongoing significance of racism" and miss the way "we inhabit cultural worlds that, in turn, promote racialized ways of seeing, being in, and acting in the world." From this perspective, instead of focusing primarily on individual manifestations of racism, "a more effectual use of personal agency may be to reconstruct worlds that promote anti-racist tendencies" (see "Racism in the Structure of Everyday Worlds: A Cultural-Psychological Perspective" by Phia S. Salter, Glenn Adam, and Michael J. Perez, Dec. 7, 2017, in *Sage* Journal).

Robin DiAngelo has added another dimension to this assessment with her recent book, *Nice Racism*. The point here is that racism will not be eradicated by Whites being "nice" to People of Color. The dismantling of the Whiteness Standard requires White people to commit to a lifetime of education and accountability in addressing embedded individual and collective racial biases. However, DiAngelo suggests that White progressives who hold liberal values and credentials have not generally developed the skills necessary for examining their role in perpetuating racial inequities and injustices. Consequently, White progressives who are empathetic to the racial oppression that People of Color often resort to expressing friendliness and respect as a means to connect with the racially marginalized and oppressed. The assumption is that moral people with good intentions can put an end to racism simply by befriending and being nice to People of Color. The critique of this individual "niceness" approach to addressing racism resides in the lack of White awareness about the systemic nature of racial biases, the pervasiveness of White privileges, a failure to appreciate racial power imbalances, and the legacy of colonization practices within White culture. Hoping to get White progressives to better align their anti-racist practice with their values, DiAngelo encourages us to start with addressing our complicity in ignoring what I have called the Whiteness Standard and embracing introspection as the way for us to notice the racial biases in ourselves and in the social and organizational structures in which we live.

One final note about our responsibility to free ourselves from our racial biases and practices comes from Heather McGhee's economic analysis of the zero-sum paradigm that assumes any racial progress made by People of Color in America will necessarily place a financial burden on Whites. In her book *The Sum of Us: What Racism Costs Everyone and How We Can Prosper Together*, she demonstrates the ways that racism exacts costs on White people and undermines our form of democracy. From her economic perspective, McGhee promotes what she calls a "solidarity dividend" when people work together across racial lines for the common benefit of all.

All of these issues should make it clear how imperative it is for us to grapple with both the social and psychological benefits that we imagine for ourselves when we cling to and celebrate our racial identity. Contending with these White emotional and ego challenges places the burden for eradicating racism in America squarely upon those of us who are White.

One of the easier ways I have found for myself to push back on our dominant culture's emphasis on racial identity is to simply stop categorizing people by "race." In that spirit, when I am asked to fill out institutional information forms, instead of identifying myself as "White" or "Caucasian," I simply write in under the race categories listed "Human." In the next chapter, I will address some of the other practical ways for Whites to engage in a conscious and intentional effort to overcome the racial biases that may reside in our institutions and in us.

CHAPTER SEVEN
FREEING OURSELVES FROM OUR WHITE RACIAL BIASES

"I only have one life that I am sure of, and as I am leaving it I want to be able to know that I did all I could do to bring about racial justice."

—Frances E. Kendall,
Understanding White Privilege: Creating Pathways to Authentic Relationships Across Race

So, how are those of us who are White supposed to confront our inherited beliefs and biases about White superiority and the White privileges that we may not even recognize within us? From what I had said thus far, it should be clear that I see two aspects to any effort to overcome the ideology of White superiority in America—one involves addressing our individual White racial biases, and the other centers on addressing institutional and systemic racism that grant privileges to Whites that are not granted to People of Color. Finding the courage to address both of these dimensions of the Whiteness Standard is essential to the kind of racism recovery process I advocate for in this book. Since latent or unrecognized ideas about White superiority continue to perpetuate institutional and systemic racism in this country, Whites must commit to purging our conscious and unconscious racial biases about skin color that we often deny, overlook, or discount. At the same time, we must also redress the many forms of institutional and systemic racism that are at work in our social, economic, religious, educational, legal, and political institutions. Soliciting the help of People of Color in these two aspects of a White racial bias recovery process is essential to this process simply because they are more aware than we are of how White biases show up in our institutions and in us.

Fortunately, there are numerous practical resources available today to help those of us who are White to learn how our embedded racial biases function to oppress People of Color and what eliminating these biases requires. Like addressing any other important challenge we may face in life, availing ourselves of these resources is an important step in expanding our understanding of the complexities of our racial biases and privileges. For those willing to seriously engage in this work, I would recommend several books that provide a comprehensive exploration into the process of overcoming White racial biases: *How To Be Less Stupid About Race* by Crystal Fleming; *Understanding and Dismantling Racism: The Twenty-First Century Challenge in America* by Joseph Barndt; or *Why Are All The Black Kids Sitting Together In The Cafeteria? And Other Conversations About Race* by Beverly Daniel Tatum. Reading any one of these books would be a good beginning point for most White people. Discussing one of these books in a book club or a book study group can often add more perspective and enhance understanding of the issue. All of these resources are just a beginning point for anyone seeking to delve into the uncomfortable arena of race and racism. Engaging in a serious racial bias recovery process will require even more intentional efforts than I am outlining here.

Beginning With Ourselves

Confronting the damaging effects of the White superiority ideology begins with an individual exploration of our racial bias and how we think about our racial identity. As I have suggested in the chapters of this book, most of us who are White need to own and recognize whatever embedded racial biases we may have. Being open to learning how our racial biases and identity show up in us without pretending that we have escaped these issues is a mandatory part of this process. There are valuable resources available today that can help individuals develop more self-awareness about our White racial prejudices and stereotypes that are unconscious as well as conscious.

One easy way to start an examination of one's inherent attitudes about race is to take one of the online Implicit Bias Tests developed by psychologists from Harvard, the University of Washington, and the University of Virginia. These tests use timed questions to unearth unconscious attitudes toward minorities, the elderly, women, and other groups. These virtual quizzes measure one's split-second reactions to a diversity of images of people. You may be surprised to discover you hold hidden White biases simply by taking one of the Harvard Implicit Association Tests on race. There are two tests on the Implicit site designed to reveal self-understanding of a personal, racial bias: the skin-tone test and the race test, both of which will indicate the level of one's preferences about skin color and racial backgrounds. While tests like these may only suggest psychological conditioning, they can help us to explore how our latent judgments affect our interactions with People of Color.

Thankfully, psychologists like Jennifer Eberhardt have provided excellent resources for understanding how unconscious biases show up in race relationships and public institutions as well (see

Biased: Uncovering the Hidden Prejudice That Shapes What We See, Think and Do, Viking Press, 2019). Another very useful resource that provides exercises aimed at exploring how to develop a non-racist White identity and combating racism can be found in Derald Wing Sue's book *Overcoming Our Racism: The Journey to Liberation* (Jossey-Bass, 2003). Again, it takes openness and courage to explore racial attitudes, reactions, and beliefs that challenge our stated values and identity.

Another excellent resource that provides an educational exploration into the issue of race is the three-episode documentary film series by California Newsreel, *Race: The Power of An Illusion.* This 2003 video resource examines the history of the race concept, the science and pseudo-science about racial identities, and the social, cultural, and institutional contexts of race in America. There is a companion website for this documentary series that provides excellent resources for further study, including a race literary quiz and race gene studies (see https://www.racepowerofanillusion.org/).

Overcoming our White innocence and naivete about inherited racial biases is also a critical challenge that many Whites have to face. Becoming more aware of how White racial biases are learned by children at an early age is both sobering and instructive (see https://www.youtube.com/watch?v=DYCz1ppTjiM&feature=youtu.be).

Recognizing how White privilege works is another challenge for many Whites. Thankfully, there are visual exercises that can help with this racial myopia (see https://www.youtube.com/watch?v=4K5fbQl-zps). Conversely, it is necessary for White people to see examples of how Black people are often treated differently and unfairly than White people of similar age and background. One case study that was done twenty years ago by a network news agency illustrates the racial disparities Blacks often encounter (see https://www.youtube.com/watch?v=oi_DF9Iu2xA). Without honest engagement with these experiences of racial biases, White people cannot develop empathy for how significant skin color is within our American culture. Whites also must learn to appreciate how racial identities have had profound effects on racial injustices and economic inequities within the past one hundred years. Most of us do not recognize how laws and social customs rooted in racism have negatively impacted People of Color as this video shows (see https://www.youtube.com/watch?v=AGUwcs9qJXY&feature=youtu.be).

To come to terms with how the Whiteness Standard operates in everyday life, anti-racism training emphasizes the value of getting Whites to watch these videos together and then have discussions about what we feel and think about examples of racial biases. Getting beyond our defensiveness about not being a racist and wanting to preserve our individual goodness as a person requires a reframing of how deeply immersed all of us are in a racist culture and system. This short video provides such a reframing of cultural racism (see https://www.youtube.com/watch?v=GnlDj1Qii8E).

Freeing ourselves from our White racial biases also requires us to confront our allegiance to our White identity and White cultural heritage. This involves the development of our emotional, intellectual, and ethical maturity as citizens of this nation in order for us to acknowledge the mistakes we have made in the past as individuals and as a predominately White culture. Owning the legacy of our nation's oppression of People of Color in the name of White superiority is part of this maturity process. Working our way out of shame, blame, and guilt for America's "original sin of racism" necessitates honesty, regret, accepting collective responsibility, and a commitment to seeking reconciliation. Guarding ourselves against the desire to preserve the virtues of being White or claiming we no longer see races are just two aspects of this process. Sometimes it is easier to see this desire to preserve White virtue in others rather than in ourselves. Comedians sometimes provide less-threatening ways to help us to recognize our White tendency to defend our cultural heritage (see John Oliver's expose on those who defend Confederate monuments as history and heritage, https://www.youtube.com/watch?v=J5b_-TZwQ0I&t=1039s).

Listening to the Experiences of Non-Whites

To move us beyond our White racial frame, our limited experiences with People of Color, and the emotional attachments most of us have to being "White," we would benefit enormously from engaging in honest dialogues about race with People of Color. Having conversations with People of Color about their experiences with racism and racial discrimination is a vital step in the process of confronting our myopia about White superiority and White privilege. When inter-racial conversations are structured around respect, honesty, and the desire to gain understanding, Whites can overcome our inability to notice how our dominant skin color affects our relationships and our social and political arrangements. People of Color usually are much more aware than we are about how the Whiteness Standard works and benefits us. Some African Americans appear to have more insight into the attitudes of White people than White people know about either People of Color or even about themselves. Dick Gregory, the African American social critic and comedian, argues that "White is not a color; it's an attitude," usually wrapped up in money and power. Gregory understands how money and power can blind us and prevent us from seeing the pain and suffering of others. Making an effort to engage in mixed-race conversations about racial biases does not come easy for White people or People of Color, due in part to a lack of trust and the impediments that our social circles create.

One of the biggest hurdles to engaging in such conversations, other than the typical isolation of Whites from non-Whites, is the tendency of Whites to want to defend our "goodness and virtues" or reassure People of Color of our good intentions. As many have noted, a key requirement for healthy conversations about race is the ability of Whites to listen empathically to People of Color for understanding without succumbing to guilt, shame, or blame. Churches and community groups who have intentionally formed mixed-race forums for dialogue about racial issues often attest to the value that such conversations can bear in changing perceptions and exposing unconscious biases, particularly for White people.

One of the most useful resources I have found to be of help in planning conversations on race in churches or community groups is *The Anti-Racist Cookbook: A Recipe Guide for Conversations About Race That Goes Beyond Covered Dishes and "Kum-Bah-Ya"* written by Robin Parker and Pamela Smith Chambers (Puffin Foundation Ltd, 2005). As this resource makes clear, developing ground rules for respectful, non-judgmental, and appreciative listening and sharing about experiences with race will be critical to productive conversations. The success of such conversations often depends on having a skilled facilitator who has some experience or a level of trust in the community to lead the conversation process. Churches can play a valuable role in creating these inter-racial conversations, particularly when predominately White congregations collaborate with congregations of Color to engage in such conversations. I have included in the appendix a series of questions around which these conversations can be structured.

Another avenue for White people to pursue in our effort to extract ourselves from White racial bias is through understanding racial identity development. Psychologists who have studied racial identities suggest that our racial identities are frequently formed in stages over time in our psychosocial development. They have discovered that the patterns of racial identity development often differ for White people and People of Color. According to White racial identity theory, those of us who are White often move from thinking we are colorblind to feeling guilt and shame when we discover the privileges of our racial identity, to blaming the victims rather than owning our racial privilege, to wanting to be both White and yet non-racist, to connecting easily with those who share our racial identity, to embracing a positive White identity committed to appreciating racial diversity. The challenge in this racial developmental process for Whites is to attain a positive racial identity without comparing ourselves to or denigrating People of Color.

Here is what one of the early developers of this theory about White racial identity says: "The task for Whites is to develop a positive White identity-based in reality, not on assumed superiority. To do that, each person must become aware of his or her Whiteness, accept it as personally and socially significant, and learn to feel good about it, not in the sense of a Klan member's 'White pride,' but in the context of a commitment to a just society" (Dr. Janet Helms as quoted in Beverly Tatum, *Why Are All the Black Kids Sitting Together in the Cafeteria?*).

Researchers have identified what they call "a color bind in America"—a condition, especially noticeable among White professionals, "wherein race is seen as an important topic yet rarely discussed in the conversation." This color bind was identified when sociologists sought to analyze how and why different teams of (mostly White) social workers in a child welfare agency either talk or do not talk about race or culture while on the job. One of their explanations for this shared color bind among people who work with minorities is due in part to "an ambivalent state that lies between individual colorblindness and color cognizance—a state they coin *color minimization* (or the acknowledgment of race but the subsequent devaluation of it because presumably some other characteristic matters more)."[1] By examining the ways different professional teams addressed race and culture issues in their work, these researchers further identified three kinds of responses among a variety of groups they studied: 1) color cognizance, 2) color avoidance, and 3) color hostility. From my experience, these are three of the most common reactions of White people to the suggestion that we need to talk about race issues.

The more honest and liberating way to move beyond today's White tendency to discount racial identities is to recognize how People of Color have been oppressed, discriminated against, marginalized, and unfairly treated in our dominant White culture. This requires the development of empathy on the part of Whites toward the victims of our racial biases. Empathy grows out of listening to and learning about the history and experiences of the victims of racial injustices and inequities at an emotional level rather than an intellectual level. Most of us who are White have been shielded from the painful history of People of Color in this nation. To expand our empathy, Whites often must intentionally learn what People of Color have experienced in America in the most graphic ways possible and identify with the feelings that come from those experiences.

One way to engage in this kind of empathy development effort is to go to places that capture the experience of non-Whites in American history. I recommend that Whites visit the National Museum of African American History and Culture in Washington, DC; the National Memorial to Peace and Justice and the Legacy Museum of Enslavement in Montgomery, Alabama; the Civil Rights Museum in Memphis, Tennessee; and a host of other sites that have collected and recorded much of this history and try to identify with the feelings of those who have been the victims of racism.

There are many other ways that Whites can develop this kind of empathy for the oppressed. Reading Black histories and the literary works of Richard Wright, Langston Hughes, James Baldwin, Toni Morrison, and Ta-Nehisi Coates also can move us in this direction, as do movies like *The Color Purple* and songs like "Strange Fruit."

The road to racial empathy will require you to hear stories about horrors of human brutality and lead you to lament the violence and inhumanity that People of Color have been subjected to for generations on end. I often wonder, however, how Whites can come to develop sufficient empathy about the destructiveness of White racism without confronting and feeling the moral failures that the ideology of White superiority has produced.

Related to this learning step in our White bias recovery process is our willingness and efforts to hear and acknowledge the unpleasant and difficult truth about America's racist history. This requires reading and listening to honest and truthful narratives about how White racial biases have shaped American life from its beginning. The most comprehensive way to learn this history is to read and discuss with others two books: Roxanne Dunbar-Ortiz's *An Indigenous People's History of the United States*, which decolonizes our nation's history from the perspective of the 15 million Indigenous humans who inhabited North America and what happened to them after the arrival of Europeans in the sixteenth century, and Ibram Kendi's award-winning *Stamped From the Beginning: The Definitive History of Racist Ideas in America*. As there are numerous other resources to help Whites come to terms with this history, I have listed some of these in the bibliography of this book.

Finding Pathways to Becoming Anti-Racists

Some Whites have reached the point where we are willing to acknowledge that serious conversations about race are necessary for our liberation from the misguided ideas about White superiority and our White privilege status. Engaging in conversations that help us to examine our perceptions about People of Color, to inquire about their experiences with White racial biases and privileges, and to strengthen our empathy takes courage and vulnerability, which may explain why many of us are reluctant to engage in conversations about racial issues. Even though "color cognizance" is the attitude that fosters the best freedom for productive conversations on race, individual ideas about race often get complicated by perceptions and ideas about cultural differences between non-Whites and Whites.

When issues of race and culture get mixed, we tend to downplay the ways that the particular histories of racial oppression in the United States matter—making racial differences less important than cultural differences. Perhaps not surprising for many White people, the recognition of a "power differential" is often left out of these conversations when White people do find the courage to talk openly about race. One good resource for examining our White disease with race can be found in a book discussion of Shelly Tochluk's *Witnessing Whiteness: First Steps Toward An Anti-Racist Practice and Culture*. As an educational psychologist, Tochluk understands the depth of commitment it takes for White people to do the self-examination and learning required for us to become anti-racists. Consequently, she advocates for Whites to participate in what I am calling a "White racism recovery group"—regular meetings where Whites come together to work on White identify issues, gain a better understanding of our embedded White biases and privileges, and learn skills to combat racism. Like most Alcohol Anonymous groups, the real test is whether enough White people can find the emotional maturity, honesty, vulnerability, and courage to participate in a structured and intentional racism recovery experience where everyone introduces themselves as a recovering racist.

Thankfully, there are now growing grassroots efforts around the U.S. for Whites and People of Color to engage in what some of us are calling "courageous conversations about race." Racial injustices in recent years have prompted a variety of small groups in communities to seek out opportunities for mixed-race conversations about racial issues in particular institutional contexts like education, civic engagement, law enforcement, economic development, etc. These localized efforts to foster and encourage racial dialogue often acknowledge that conversations about race are difficult for many of the reasons discussed in this book. Creating safe environments for honest and respectful discussions is a key component in many of these efforts to discuss openly individual perceptions about our racial differences and encourage mutual learning experiences.

The value of speaking for oneself and listening carefully without judgment to the experience of others is emphasized in these conversations about race. Acknowledging distrust among our various racial groups sometimes has to be addressed. Learning to "speak one's truth in love" is frequently emphasized and modeled in such conversations. Resources for these types of "courageous conversations on race" can be found in consulting services pioneered by Glenn Singleton with seminars on Beyond Diversity (see https://courageousconversation.com/), in the Undoing Racism programs and workshops conducted by the People's Institute for Survival and Beyond (see https://www.pisab.org/about-us/), or other trained consultants organizations that provide implicit bias training.

The work of dismantling racism requires White people to be clear about their intentions, avoid micro-aggressions against People of Color, and practice humility when engaging both Whites and non-Whites in hopes of building collaborative partnerships that affirm the humanity of all. Well-intending Whites need to learn how to become a "White ally" without working against this goal by trying to "fix the racial problems of others," convincing others of our "wokeness," or suggesting strategies to end racism for good. Without this learning orientation and checking against our White innocence or over-confidence, we often commit "micro-aggressions" when we make unexamined statements, actions, or behave in ways that communicate indirect, subtle, or unintentional discrimination against People of Color. To emphasize the importance of this type of effort and how we might best become a White ally, I will address the issue in the next chapter.

Let me emphasize here the importance of engaging in this work with humility. As I have noted, my approach to overcoming racism and racial bias issues is rooted in my orientation as a person of faith who appreciates the value of acknowledging our failures, mistakes, and culpability in restoring our broken relationships with others. My experience in ministry has taught me that people rarely become moral or more empathetic to others simply by someone pointing out their ethical failures or by urging them to be better people. Most positive change within people usually comes from a personal engagement with an ideal we seek to embody. My faith tradition has led me to believe in the value of self-examination when it comes to living out our ideals. Such self-examination often leads to confessions about our failure to embody our ideals, and confession often leads to repentance, and repentance leads to a changed heart and mind.

This religious orientation has impressed upon me the importance of acknowledging my racial biases, however subtle these may be, as a critical step in overcoming the embedded influences of the Whiteness Standard that still inhabits my life on occasion. Confessing our racial biases, whether great or small, requires us to take personal responsibility for the residual racism or unconscious White biases that may still inhabit our attitudes and behaviors with regard to relating to non-Whites. It seems to me that a key to overcoming racism in America begins with our ability to acknowledge our nation's racist past, confess our self-justifications and our tendencies to exonerate both ourselves and White America for these moral failures, and confront our White denial about the corrosive impact that the ideology of White superiority has had on race relations in our country from its beginning. For many Whites, this may be the penultimate challenge in dismantling the legacy of racism in America.

Looking Beyond Individual White Racial Biases

Those of us who profess to be socially minded and committed to the common good of all will also need to recognize the pervasiveness of the institutional or systemic sins that are embedded in America's political, economic, legal, and educational structures. As one Unitarian Universalist pastor has observed, many of us are eager to legislate an end to racial bias in policing but less eager to police the racial bias in our collective psyches. There is in all of us some personal culpability for the evils of the ideology of White supremacy that resides in political, social, legal, and economic structures that provide advantages for Whites while disadvantaging People of Color.

So, I believe we must address the racial biases and the White privileges that exist in the institutional policies and practices of our nation. My experience tells me that owning our complicity in a racist system is extremely difficult for most of us who are White, simply because we are unaware of the institutional and structural dimensions of White racial biases. Some of us have come to appreciate the efforts of those like Harvard's professor of history, Louis Henry Gates, who uses genealogical research to "deconstruct the idea of racial purity" in America by recognizing both the historical struggles with racial identities in our shared history and how this history has shaped all of us. Recognizing the patterns of structural racism in the history of our nation will enable us to understand and work to dismantle the oppression of non-Whites today.

The Teaching Tolerance curriculum developed by the Southern Poverty Law Center attempts to help Whites recognize the ingrained institutional biases that have to be addressed to eliminate racism. Once again, the burden for this antiracism work is placed on White people who have created and benefit from these institutionalized racial biases. Anti-racist work asks us to acknowledge that racist beliefs and structures are pervasive in all aspects of our lives—from education to housing to climate change—and then actively take action to tear down those beliefs and structures. Racist beliefs and structures don't just exist in primarily White and/or privileged institutions—they thrive there.

Schools, for example, that are comprised mostly of students and teachers who have benefited from White privilege often lack the perspective to notice and confront institutional malpractice or racist mindsets that may be present. It is even more difficult to convince those with power and privilege to give those privileges up without providing them with an understanding of why doing so is a necessity for true justice in our society. To address internalized racial biases and racial traumas, there is a genre of books and resources generally aimed at "healing the racial divide in America" (see, for example, *The Racial Healing Handbook: Practical Activities to Help You Challenge Privilege, Confront Systemic Racism, and Engage in Collective Healing* by Anneliese A. Singh, PhD, LPC). Many of these resources focus on the psychodynamics of racism and its effects on individuals, relationships, and communities.

As I have stated in previous chapters, confronting structural and institutional racial biases places a particular burden on Whites because we will be asked to take personal action to address racial issues or problems that exist around us, particularly when our lives are not directly impacted by those issues or problems. Asking Whites to take action to address social and political issues in America brings many of us up against apathy and pessimism about effecting constructive change in institutions that are beyond our spheres of influence. Moreover, many of us believe the common good will be best served when individuals are working to achieve their own self-interests, without harming others and with the approval of the majority. The idealized presumption in this philosophy is that "all of us are created equal," and we all have equal opportunities to pursue life, liberty, and happiness. It is easy for most of us who have bought into this philosophy to attribute the successes and failures of individuals and even groups of people to their own initiatives and efforts.

So, some Whites will continue to believe that every individual is responsible for having a fruitful, productive, and self-sufficient life. This idea of personal responsibility comes up frequently in conversations about racial disparities or racial injustices when there is little appreciation among Whites for the disadvantages that non-Whites have lived under for generations. Productive conversations about racial biases, however, should include a recognition that People of Color have not been accorded equal opportunities to Whites in the course of our nation's history so that accumulated wealth, better educational opportunities, and White privileges have kept the racial playing field from being level. Otherwise, at-tributing racial disparities to individual initiative and effort will sound like blaming the victims of racism. I believe that for Whites to address the structural and institutional racial biases that exist in America, we will need to find an ethical motivation that tran-scends the apathy, pessimism, and indifference that many of us have about affecting needed social, economic, or political changes.

Acknowledging the Benefits of Whiteness

The resistance many White people feel and express about the idea of "White privilege" also has to be addressed clearly and forth-rightly. Most White people simply do not see any benefit in our social status granted to us simply by the dominant color of our skin. Somewhat surprisingly, many of us today are now willing to acknowledge that men have long been given preferential treatment over women in the workplace, positions of power, and other struc-tures of our so-called equal society. But at the same time, many of us are blind as to how skin color provides us with more access, easier acceptance, or greater acceptance in the social, economic, and political structures in which we live.

One of the ways that our local Courageous Conversations group has approached the idea of "White privilege" is to invite a racial-ly mixed group of folks to participate in a cultural competency training experience where we explore together the dynamics of racial biases at both the personal and the institutional level. One exercise that demonstrates how White privilege works is to line all the participants up at one end of a large room with instructions to take two steps forward whenever an individual can affirm one of a series of statements that are asked of the group. Finding opportunities to participate in these kinds of local or national cultural competency training experiences will take some effort and commitment of time and money on the part of most Whites. A couple of examples of the type of training to address White privilege can be found at https://www.racialequitytools.org/curricula/transforming-white-privilege and justiceandrenewal.org. There are many other opportunities that can be found simply by doing an internet search for "racial awareness training," "racial sensitivity training," or "antiracism training."

Apologizing for White Racism, Past and Present

From the start of this book, I have advocated for Whites to accept the responsibility, both individually and collectively, for the sins of racism. When our nation was rocked by the racial injustices in the first half of 2020 with the deaths of Breonna Taylor, Amaud Arbery, George Floyd, and Rashayd Brooks, many of us found ourselves grieving the horrors and inhumanity of racism, police brutality, and violence that took their lives. The video recordings and news reports about the murders of numerous unarmed Black people and attacks on Asian Americans have shaken our moral sensibilities and exposed the contradictions in our stated social and moral values. Some of us have joined People of Color in expressing outrage about these racial injustices via protests and calls for defunding the police. Others of us have attended racial awareness opportunities and supported the Black Lives Matter movement. A few of us have become supporters of a national reparation initiative.

In the aftermath of the murder of George Floyd, a group of our White friends in our community felt compelled to offer an apology to our friends of color for our complicity in the systems of White superiority and privilege that gave rise to these racial tragedies. For me, it's troubling that our nation has never apologized to Native Americans, African Americans, Latino Americans, or Asian Americans for the sins of racism in America's past. Without honest confession of our mistakes in clinging to the ideology of White superiority and White privilege, we are unlikely to ever heal the racial divide in America. Many faith traditions have emphasized the necessity of confronting our mistakes and seeking forgiveness for our moral failures but rarely has this call for repentance and atonement entered into our national conversation about racial justice.

As Susan Neiman has observed in her book *Learning from the Germans: Race and the Memory of Evil*, our nation might benefit from confronting the sins of our racist past in the same way that Germany confronted the horrors of the Holocaust in the 1960s. The term they used for engaging in this effort to move beyond unsaid guilt and unsaid resentment is translated as "working off the past." Rather than seeking to reconstruct their national identity, Germany decided to memorialize the victims of the Nazi brutality and inhumanity as a means of atonement. I hope to live to see the day our nation can find the fortitude and moral convictions to do the same with regard to America's racist past.

But this White indifference to our nation's racist past and the denial about this racial legacy of White superiority is in itself telling. The resistance among some White people to acknowledging this history continues to show up in many forms: among those White people who purport to honor their Southern heritage but disavow hate; those of us who insist that acknowledging our nation's racist history does nothing to improve race relations or the plight of African

Americans today; those who argue that removing or questioning Confederate monuments and Confederate heroes is an attempt to erase or re-write history; and those who dismiss the idea that we must face the legacy of slavery and racism as America's "original sin" because even our nation's heroes like Jefferson and Lincoln believed in White supremacy and should not be judged by today's standards. Today, we are hearing calls for replacing the teaching about the history of racism in the U.S. with "patriot education" that emphasizes American exceptionalism, presumably to preserve the virtues of the White founders of our nation and their progeny. I believe it is time for Whites who want to be anti-racists to confront and reject this kind of White denial about the legacy of racism in our country.

Working on Our White Empathy Deficits

So, what can we do to purge the disease of White superiority from our White souls? I don't recall where I read this, but it captures for me a "meanwhile" ethic: "While recognizing the schizophrenia of those who cherish most the 'superiority' of White men, we need not be paralyzed by it. While we attempt to cure the sick and educate the ignorant, the law and the courts must confine the insane [Whites] and protect the victims." I have found that educating ourselves about the history of slavery, the racial discrimination and injustices institutionalized in Jim Crow laws, and the struggles of the civil rights era can be valuable aids for coming to terms with the disease of White superiority in this country.

In 2018, my wife and I organized a chartered bus trip for a mixed-race and multigenerational group in our community to travel to Selma and Montgomery, Alabama, to experience some of the iconic sites of the civil rights movement and to visit the new National Memorial to Peace and Justice and the Legacy Museum. On this "Riding the Freedom Trail" trip, we asked our group to watch videos of the 1963 Bloody Sunday march on the Edmund Pettus Bridge in Selma and the march to Montgomery. In Selma, we learned about Jim Crow laws that prevented African Americans from voting, and we heard a civil rights pioneer tell us about her experience with the marches in the 1960s. This experience was especially educative for the high school and college students who were on this journey with us and had not lived through the civil rights era. We walked together over the Edmund Pettus Bridge, singing "We Shall Overcome" and stopping for a prayer that was offered by one of our college students. In Montgomery, we visited the Rosa Parks Museum, the Freedom Riders Museum, the Southern Poverty Law Center, and the Legacy Enslavement Museum.

After worship on Sunday at the King Memorial Dexter Avenue Baptist Church, we went to the National Memorial to Peace and Justice to witness the thousands of memorials erected there to lynched victims of racial discrimination and injustice during the Jim Crow era. In the evenings, our group engaged in honest conversations about what we had seen and learned from each day's activities. Most of the Whites on this trip acknowledged the pain and remorse they felt from the historical reminders of the suffering that African Americans have experienced at the hands of White racists. Most of the People of Color shared the grief they felt for the suffering their ancestors experienced from racial violence and discrimination, as well as an appreciation for their resilience in the face of such hardships and injustices. We came away from this journey recognizing that, for those of us who are White, this was an important exercise in working on what Bryon Stevenson calls our "empathy deficit" regarding the oppressive racial experiences of African Americans in this country. Naming and claiming the destructiveness of the ideology of White superiority is part of this racial reconciliation process for Whites in particular.

As I suspect my confession of racism has revealed, freeing ourselves from the ideology of White superiority requires a great deal of introspection, moral honesty, and a desire to work at purging ourselves from this insidious social disease. Since my racist belief in White superiority was largely a learned experience from childhood, my recovery from racism has been a matter of unlearning old ideas and affirming new understandings about myself and people with different skin colors. This has been a lifelong journey for me. Old habits and ideas are hard to change when we have benefited in some way from them unconsciously, socially, and materially. Because racial identity so often involves matters of the heart and not just our thinking, I have discovered that attending to old, misguided feelings about People of Color is also part of the recovery process. This is where developing honest relationships with People of Color becomes crucial in this process. Listening to People of Color about their experiences with racism, talking with other White about our racial biases and assumptions, offering apologies for our complicity in not challenging institutional racism, and inviting and receiving feedback on our viewpoints on race are all critical to this healing work.

Working on Behalf of Racial Justice and Equity

As I have tried to explain from my own experience, dismantling racism in America will require more than changing the hearts and minds of White people in order to purge ourselves of our White racial biases. While we must engage in our individual racial transformation work, it will likely take generations of White people striving to remove our racial biases before we come to appreciate living in a racially and culturally diverse society without People of Color being oppressed in some way. Meanwhile, the best collective strategy I see available to counter residual and hidden White racism involves our efforts to dismantle the structural and systemic forms of White superiority and privilege that are embedded in our economic, social, educational, legal, religious, and political institutions.

As I have already noted about White privilege, most White people are oblivious to and unaffected by the dynamics of institutionalized White racial biases. Learning from the experiences of People of Color is critical for Whites to gain an understanding of how the Whiteness Standard shows up and operates within our society. One of the common refrains among African American advocates of cross-cultural community organizing is the urging of White people to divest ourselves of our White power and privileges. Relinquishing our White power and privileges stand as very hard challenges for many Whites who do not see or accept the idea that racial biases continue to grant advantages to Whites while disadvantaging People of Color. Learning how institutionalized racial biases and privileges are built into the fabric of our society is a critical step on the path toward working for racial justice and equity.

Once Whites become aware of the institutional and structural manifestations of White racial biases, we must make an effort to redress the racial inequities that are embedded in many of our nation's public and corporate policies and practices. As People of Color have been suggesting for decades now, this work will require the White divestment of power and control in our nation's institutions. For this White divestment of power to occur, we will need to embrace a collective appreciation for the cultural differences that affirms "White is not always equated with right." Until White people who control the power structures in government, education, and business are willing to engage in implicit bias training and learn how the dynamics of White power and privilege show up in our institutional policies and practices, we are not likely to recognize the advantages we have from just having White skin, nor increase racial equities. Just as individual Whites must work at increasing our empathy deficits toward People of Color, our social, economic, educational, and political institutions will have to confront and change embedded and hidden White racial biases that permeate our institutions and social structures.

In addition to divesting ourselves of the institutional White power structures that create disadvantages for People of Color, I believe we must also acknowledge the limitations and handicaps that Whites have historically placed on non-Whites over the ages. To this end, Whites should find ways to invest in organizations that empower People of Color with educational opportunities, job training and economic development initiatives, patronize non-White businesses, provide support for civic leadership for People of Color, and find other means to influence social policies and practices that benefit racial minorities.

To close the gaps of White institutionally sanctioned advantages and to foster more racial equity today, I firmly believe that our nation will have to honestly recognize the generational effects of racism and establish some measure of reparations for People of Color. As Martin Luther King, Jr. argued at the end of his life, "Letting Negroes sit at lunch counters didn't cost the country a dime." But, as he noted, "Promoting economic justice and freedom for People of Color will cost this nation billions of dollars."

As Joe Feagin points out in his book *Racist America: Roots, Current Realities, and Future Reparations*, few of us seem ready today to make material restitution for our nation's past racial injustices and inequalities. He notes that both the U.S. Senate and House of Representatives passed "resolutions" in 2008 to apologize "to African Americans on behalf of the people of the United States, for the wrongs committed against them and their ancestors who suffered under slavery and Jim Crow laws." However, this modest apology was followed by a provision that prevented African Americans from seeking government reparations for generations of oppression.

In recent years, a number of strong cases have been made to consider a national reparations effort for both African American and Indigenous American descendants (see https://www.theatlantic.com/magazine/archive/2014/06/the-case-for-reparations/361631/; https://www.brookings.edu/policy2020/bigideas/why-we-need-reparations-for-black-americans/; https://www.npr.org/2020/06/24/882773218/a-call-for-reparations-how-america-might-narrow-the-racial-wealth-gap).

In April 2021, the House of Representatives approved a bill, H. R. 40, that would create a thirteen-member commission charged with studying the causes of racial discrimination and disenfranchisement of Black voters, dating back to the nation's history of slavery. This committee will also present proposals of rehabilitation and restitution to Congress. Given the current Republican opposition to such proposals and their efforts to further disenfranchise People of Color from voting in the name of election security, the idea of reparations for racial injustices will likely face enormous opposition within large segments of the White population. Feagin's book provides arguments on behalf of a national restitution and reparations effort, along with other anti-racist strategies, like instituting educational courses of racism, holding a U.S. Constitutional Convention to address human rights, and Affirmative Action policies and remedial racial equity initiatives.

With the political polarization we have in America today, I believe addressing these kinds of strategies will gain the most support and impact at the local level before achieving state or national level support. The challenge is for Whites at the local level to take up these kinds of initiatives via collaborating with racial justice initiatives and community organizing efforts.

One of the ways some of us have moved toward addressing institutional racism in our community has been through the development of our Courageous Conversations group. Through this interracial community project initiated by faith community leaders, educators, and community activists in our city, we have been working together to create Dr. King's vision of the Beloved Community locally. As I have noted, this initiative began with open and honest conversations about racial equity and justice issues among group members wanting to build trust and understanding among us. Once we had established mutual trust and respect, we turned our attention to addressing racial justice and equity issues that involved affordable housing, public safety, job training and living wages, public school equity, and access to health care. The centerpiece of this Courageous Conversations effort has been a shared commitment to fulfilling Dr. King's vision of the Beloved Community in our small town in Texas. After every meeting, we join together in sharing our commitments by reciting the following:

An Affirmation of Faith Based on the Writings of Dr. Martin Luther King Jr.

I refuse to believe that we are unable to influence the events that surround us.

I refuse to believe that we are so bound to racism and war that peace, brotherhood, and sisterhood are not possible.

I believe that there is an urgent need for people to overcome oppression and violence without resorting to violence and oppression.

I believe that we need to discover a way to live together in peace, a way that rejects revenge, aggression, and retaliation. The foundation of this way is love.

I believe that unarmed truth and unconditional love will have the final word in reality. I believe that right temporarily defeated is stronger than evil triumphant.

I believe that people everywhere can have three meals a day for their bodies, education and culture for their minds, and dignity, equality, and freedom for their spirits.

I believe that what self-centered people have torn down, other-centered people can build up.

By the goodness of God at work within people, I believe that brokenness can be healed, "And the lion and the lamb shall lie down together, and everyone will sit under their own vine and fig tree, and none shall be afraid."

I believe that shared affirmations like these are important in our efforts to overcome racism in America.

CHAPTER EIGHT
BECOMING A WHITE ALLY

"Still, as I look at his picture, it is the man and not the icon that speaks to me. I cannot swallow whole the view of Lincoln as the Great Emancipator. As a law professor and civil rights lawyer and as an African American, I am fully aware of his limited views on race. Anyone who actually reads the Emancipation Proclamation knows it was more a military document than a clarion call for justice. Scholars tell us too that Lincoln wasn't immune from political considerations and that his temperament could be indecisive and morose. But it is precisely those imperfections— and the painful self-awareness of those failings etched in every crease of his face and reflected in those haunted eyes—that make him so compelling. For when the time came to confront the greatest moral challenge this nation has ever faced, this all too human man did not pass the challenge on to future generations."
—President Barack Obama reflecting on the portrait of President Abraham Lincoln on the 200th anniversary of Lincoln's birth.

Let's assume for a moment that you recognize the pervasiveness of White racial biases and privileges in our American culture, and you realize that all of us who are White need to work at freeing ourselves and our nation's institutions of both our conscious and unconscious, embedded White racial biases. As I have argued, this in itself is a critical recognition that escapes most White people today. Once we come to this awareness, committing ourselves to dismantle racism requires us to find the intellectual and emotional courage to take personal responsibility for freeing ourselves from whatever residuals of White superiority ideologies, White privileges, and latent racial biases we discover within us.

As we go about this personal challenge to root out our own embedded racial biases and behaviors, we must also work on eradicating the Whiteness standard from the institutional policies and practices that continue to discriminate against and create disadvantages for People of Color in this country. Overcoming the White structural biases embedded in America's institutions will require as much attention and effort as individual Whites must give to purging ourselves of our racial biases. For this collective effort to occur, I believe that two psychosocial dynamics of "cultural Whiteness" must be addressed: (a) White egoism and (b) White pride.

By "White egoism," I mean the accumulated cultural experience and desire among White people to control our environment and demonstrate that we can and should fix any problem we face. In short, most White people are accustomed to thinking that we have the right to express our opinions, be listened to and respected, and expect that others know we have good intentions. The prevalence of White power and pride has never been questioned in this country in the way that Black power and pride were in the 1970s and 1980s. Unlike other racial identities, the virtues of White racial identity have long been assumed in America. White people are accustomed to seeing those who look like us in leadership roles, making institutional decisions, speaking with authority, and having the power to shape public policies and civic life. Our cultural Whiteness Standard makes it difficult for most of us to take the posture of listening and learning from People of Color or expecting a Person of Color to be as capable as a White person in providing institutional leadership. This "White egoism" shows up in conversations today about race in the form of White micro-aggressions and White racial vanity (for a parody of these tendencies, see this video on "Whitesplaining," see https://www.youtube.com/watch?v=N-p8dOqf3P4). This cultural Whiteness can also be seen in the White pushback against the Black Lives Matter movement when we insist that "all lives matter."

Similarly, "White pride" is the cultural linking of the best values, the highest moral and educational achievements, the acceptable social norms and status, and the best artist expressions to White people and communities. This adulation of White cultural values and achievements has a subtle way of implying that People of Color need to live up to our Whiteness Standards and conform to White ways of functioning in the world. In most cases, White cultural pride and power serve to enhance notions about White superiority and to marginalize the contributions and gifts of non-Whites. Both White egoism and White pride tend to conspire against the empowerment of People of Color in leadership roles and in hearing their critiques of inequitable social, economic, and political arrangements that favor Whiteness. I believe these two cultural Whiteness needs explain in large measure the White resistance to affirmative action measures, the White outrage about protests against racial injustices by People of Color, and the resistance to the idea of offering a national apology and making reparations for America's sins of racism.

To move beyond our tendencies to maintain our cultural Whiteness, I think that most White people would better serve racial justice and equity goals today by becoming "White allies." The easiest way Whites can express our allyship with People of Color is simply by breaking the silence that frequently exists within White communities about race issues. As I have noted in previous chapters, White fragility and discomfort in talking about racism often cause us to avoid the subject, even with other Whites. As Dr. Martin Luther King, Jr. pointed out in his "Letter from the Birmingham Jail" to White clergy who complained about his racial justice activity in their city, the struggle to overcome racism is not confined to the hateful words and actions of some White people. King suggested that many Whites are complicit in perpetuating racism via "the appalling silence of the good people." Those of us who are White must break the White silence about racial issues. Finding the courage to raise racial justice issues within our White communities, challenge White defensiveness and privileges when we see or hear it expressed, and share our perspectives on dismantling racism with other Whites constitute a pragmatic way for us to escape complicity and become anti-racists.

At this point in our nation's history, I firmly believe that a commitment to working on behalf of racial justice and equity will require more Whites to let go of certain economic and political assumptions and benefits. Many of us will have to stop believing that free-market capitalism will solve the affordable housing crisis, the health care crisis, the environmental crisis, or any of the other common good challenges we now face in America. More of us will need to stop participating in self-interested consumerist practices that contribute to low-wage jobs and gross pay inequities in businesses and corporations. More Whites will have to stop blaming People of Color for the gaps in wealth, income, education, health, and political representation that now exist in this nation. Many more of us need to stop supporting political candidates who want to suppress voting rights that disproportionately impact People of

Color in order to maintain political power. Far more of us must stop ignoring the institutional abuses, practices, and failures that have a greater negative impact on People of Color than Whites. Those who aspire to be anti-racists must stop dismissing or excusing the White cultural racists who see People of Color and those of different ethnic backgrounds as a problem rather than an asset for America. Confronting these manifestations of systemic, institutional, and cultural racism are critical aspects of using our White power and influence to achieve greater racial equity and justice.

David Campt, an African American racial equity advocate, has suggested that Whites can play a significant role in overcoming racism and racial injustices by challenging other White people to confront their racial biases and White privilege. He argues that this is the defining characteristic of a "White ally" working for racial inclusion and justice. In his *White Ally Toolkit*, Campt argues that future racial progress will best be achieved through conversations among White people "who know that racism is a special burden on POC and who think that racism affects every group equally." To relieve People of Color from the fatigue of educating White people about the dynamics of racism, he advocates for racially aware Whites to take the initiative to engage other Whites in conversations built around active listening, empathy, and personal storytelling in order to promote racial equity. Campt encourages White allies to talk with our relatives, neighbors, colleagues, and associates about racial issues with what he calls "dialogic engagement" rather than confronting them with hard truths about White racism and how White biases harm People of Color. By taking White fragility seriously, this approach to racial awareness building among Whites emphasizes the effective communication strategies that draw White people out about how they feel about race, racism, and White privilege while avoiding condemnation or implying we are more racially "woke."

In his instructional workbook, Campt begins by asking White allies to do their own personal assessment of our own attitudes and beliefs about racial issues in order to develop the capacity for empathy toward Whites who may be less open or aware of racial biases. He outlines what he calls "the RACE method," an anacronym for Reflect, Ask, Connect, and Expand, to help other Whites explore in a non-threatening way the exchange of information, experiences, and perceptions about race issues and White racial biases. Serving as a "primer" for Whites who are willing to start race conversations with other Whites, his workbook provides instructional guidance for addressing definitions and key concepts like "unconscious bias," "unearned racial advantage," "institutional racism," and "racial equity." Campt makes the interesting point that the antiracism movement in America today doesn't really know which Whites are better served in racial awareness-building—either those who are invited to share together personal stories about racism or those asked to address community and institutional racial issues. Consequently, White allies will need to determine what strategies and approaches work best for us and for those we might engage about racial issues.

There are, of course, many constructive ways that Whites can and should work with People of Color to dismantle racism. One important way for us to become "White allies" is to follow the lead of People of Color in deciding who, when, what, and how to address racial issues. Giving up our White power and pride seems to me to be an essential part of this kind of White allyship. In addition to the lack of White self-awareness about our own embedded racial biases, one of the frequent blind spots among potential White allies is a lack of humility with regard to judgments about who among us is "woke" or not about White racial biases. As David Campt notes, some of us who recognize the dynamics of White racism and privilege often try to demonstrate to People of Color that we are among the racially enlightened White people. I have also discovered that some of us on this journey to free ourselves of White racial biases and to create racial justice can become judgmental about both the poor self-awareness of other Whites and the efforts others are making to promote racial equity. Thinking of ourselves as recovering racists can help us develop humility about our own liberation from racism and enable us to appreciate the efforts that others are making to dismantle racism as well. Dismantling racism will require us to become allies with other Whites who are working on addressing their racial biases and White privilege as well as working with People of Color. At the same time, I believe most of us who are White should be willing to support businesses run by People of Color, contribute to causes that advocate for People of Color, and look for ways to invest in the future of Children of Color.

This brings us to one of the biggest challenges in becoming White allies, especially in terms of eradicating institutional and systemic racism. Most Whites have a blind spot that prevents us from recognizing the myriad ways institutional and systemic racism are embedded in our nation's social, political, educational, and economic structures. We also have to recognize the racial power differential that Whites embody and the ways we are accustomed to functioning in our daily lives. Rather than assume we know how to best go about addressing embedded White racial biases with individuals or within institutions, White allies often are asked to become followers rather than leaders. This requires us to join organizations led by People of Color, respecting their wisdom and the priorities they set for addressing institutional change, and sustaining our engagement in these efforts. Developing the trust of People of Color is an important element in becoming a White ally. Taking a learning posture when working collaboratively with People of Color and demonstrating that we want to be held accountable for our behavior will move us toward developing authentic relationships of mutuality with People of Color. Most well-intentioned White allies will, at one time or another, have to resist our desire to be "the great White hope" in community efforts to address racism.

Finally, White allies need to recognize the social costs that will come with our antiracism efforts. White allies cannot sit on the sidelines and let others do all the heavy lifting that is necessary for challenging institutional and systemic racism. White allies will have to risk being alienated from friends and family when we confront the racial biases we hear or see going on in these relationships. White allies have to find the courage to speak out publicly to challenge racist institutional policies and practices. White allies will have to be willing to lose personal status, economic benefits, and certain privileges that might result when we call for changes within White power structures and White-controlled institutions. The old story about a pig and a chicken talking about making a contribution to someone's bacon and egg breakfast reveals the costs that White allies often will have to make in dismantling racism. The pig realized that the chicken was making only a contribution to the breakfast while the pig was being asked to make a total sacrifice.

In taking on this kind of racism recovery effort, many of us sometimes need to be inspired by others who have found the fortitude to confront their own racial biases and to work toward ending systemic racial injustices and inequalities. This has certainly been true for me. For example, the courageous stands taken by Judge J. Waties Waring in the 1940s and 1950s in South Carolina have been a wonderful source of inspiration for my racial allyship with People of Color. As a White federal judge who was born and educated in Charleston, Waring became an unlikely and locally unpopular civil rights advocate with his rulings on court cases involving racial justice issues. Standing on his moral principles regarding the law,

Judge Waring, an eighth-generation Charlestonian and son of a Confederate veteran whose family had once owned slaves, withstood the intense White bigotry, threats from the KKK, and the harsh social backlash against his court rulings on behalf of equal rights for Negroes. Along the way, he became friends with many prominent African American leaders of his day when he and his wife moved to New York, and he was given an honorary doctorate by Howard University for his allyship with African Americans. After offering the dissenting opinion in the landmark *Briggs v. Elliott* case, Waring proclaimed that "the cancer of segregation will never be cured by the sedative of gradualism" within White attitudes.

To learn what White allyship may entail, I encourage the reading of one of several books about J. Waties Waring: *In Darkest South Carolina: J. Waties Waring and the Secret Plan that Sparked a Civil Rights Movement* by Brain Hicks (2018); *Unexampled Courage: The Blinding of Sgt. Isaac Woodard and the Awakening of President Harry S. Truman and Judge J. Waties Waring* by Richard Gergel (2019); or *A Passion for Justice: J. Waties Waring and Civil Rights* by Tinsley E. Yarbrough (1987).

As I hope my confession about being a recovering racist implies, most of us who are White need all the help we can get to become White allies and anti-racists in the life of this nation.

EPILOGUE

I took a colleague's students into the Jim Crow Museum. I showed them the ugliness, the Mammy, the Sambo, the Brute, the caricatured sores foisted on black Americans. I showed them. Showed it all. And we went deep, deeper than ever before, deeper than I meant to go. My anger showed. After three hours they left, all but two -- a young black woman and a middle-aged white man. The woman sat, paralyzed, transfixed, and stunned before a picture of four naked black children. The children sat on a riverbank. At the bottom of the picture were these words: "Alligator Bait." She sat there, watching it, trying to understand the hand that had made it, the mind that conceived it. She did not say a word, but her eyes, her frown, the hand at her forehead all said, "Why, sweet Jesus, why?" The white man stopped staring at the items and stared at me. He was crying. Not a sob, a single tear stream. His tears moved me. I walked toward him. Before I could talk, he said, "I am sorry,

Mr. Pilgrim. Please forgive me." He had not created the racist
objects in the room, but he had benefited from living in a society
where blacks were oppressed. Racial healing follows sincere
contrition. I never realized how much I needed to hear some
white person, any sincere white person, say, "I am sorry, forgive
me." I wanted and needed an apology -- a heartfelt one that
changes two lives. His words took the steam out of my anger.

—Jim Pilgrim, Curator, Jim Crow Museum,
Ferris State University

I finished writing this book in the aftermath of the murder of
George Floyd in Minneapolis and the trial of the police officer
who caused his death. Since then, several more unarmed African
Americans have been shot by police in what appears in social media
videos to be the unnecessary use of force. This litany of police violence against black men, along with the white vigilante murder of
Armaud Arbery and the racist rant of Amy Cooper in Central Park
in New York City, have now awakened many Whites to the racial inequities and injustices that People of Color have endured for ages.

The news reports about the disproportionate deaths of BIPOC
from the Covid-19 epidemic in 2020 have also made more White
Americans empathetic to the racial disparities that continue to
show up in our nation. Many more of us have begun to understand
why so many People of Color are tired and angry about this unrelenting White racism that negatively impacts their lives. Some
of us are now expressing public solidarity with the Black Lives
Matter movement. In some respects, our entire nation has been
sensitized in this past year alone to the racial inequalities and injustices that we have otherwise ignored for decades. The question
now is what those of us who are White will actively do, if anything,
to address the persistence of racial inequalities and injustice.

There are some hopeful signs that more Whites in this country will be motivated to address the age-old Color line problem in America that W. E. B. Dubois pointed out more than one hundred years ago. Some of us are looking for ways to become "anti-racists" or White allies with People of Color. Historians and schoolteachers are beginning to address more directly the ugly and ignored history of racism that was woven into the fabric of this nation from its beginning. Faith communities, universities, and public libraries have started to develop webinars and virtual programs to engage in conversations about eradicating racism and promoting racial equity. As we moved through the 2020 election year and the pandemic, concerns about racial issues have surfaced more often in our public conversations. Black professional athletes have used their sports status to call attention to the racial problems that White America has wanted to ignore. All of these are indications to me of a new willingness and urgency around our country to finally come to terms with the White racial biases that have oppressed non-Whites for the past four hundred years on this continent. We shall see in the years ahead how dedicated White people and White-controlled institutions in this country really are to eradicating racial injustices and inequities.

This much seems to be clear—eliminating White racial biases will require many more Whites to examine and remove our deeply embedded individual racial biases before we can achieve the kind of racial justice and equity we claim to be seeking. As today's anti-racist advocates are suggesting, the proof of this White racial cleansing will be evident only when racist public policies and practices are removed in order to establish racial equity and justice policies and practices. This may be the pivotal challenge that White America must struggle to achieve.

As I have attempted to argue from my own experience, confessing our individual White racial biases and seeking to reconstruct our White identity is critical to meeting the host of challenges our nation must continue to address to achieve liberty and justice for all. In my view, the road to racial equity and justice will require us as a nation to apologize for the racist sins of our past and to seek reparations for People of Color in order to close the economic, legal, educational, and political gaps that now exist between Whites and non-Whites in this country. With all these challenges before us, I find myself wondering if enough White people in America will find the moral strength and political courage that is needed to travel down this long and rocky road to racial equality.

The substance of this challenge to America has been clear now for more than fifty years. Dr. Martin Luther King, Jr. expressed this challenge in his "I Have a Dream" speech that he delivered in Washington, DC, in 1963. His speech was instrumental in raising the racial consciousness of White America by exposing the disparities that exist between our nation's stated ideals and the realities of racial segregation and discrimination that were present everywhere in America at that time. King's speech about securing racial justice for People of Color contained this haunting question that he had often heard White people raise about the efforts of the civil rights movement to overcome racial discrimination: "When will you be satisfied?" In response to this question, Dr. King offered a series of social and political restraints that White racial biases had placed on People of Color, and he concluded that we should never be satisfied until all of those restraints have been completely removed.

So, as we engage in today's ongoing racism recovery process, we should not be satisfied with eliminating just overt White racial biases or reducing racial inequities for People of Color in our criminal justice system, as important as these are. In this book, I have argued that the racial equality and justice ideals facing us today revolve around the unfinished work White people need to do to overcome the persistently arrogant belief that light skin colors somehow reflect a higher human value and destiny than darker skin colors. So, we must not be satisfied as a nation until this pernicious belief about White racial superiority and control has been purged from our collective social consciousness as well as from our economic, political, and educational institutions. The accompanying loss of White privileges will be difficult for many of us. And only BIPOC will be able to tell us when this has been achieved. In a larger sense, eradicating racism in America is a necessary and needed requirement for our nation to exemplify the Democratic principles and values we claim America is based upon.

For a number of years now, our local MLK Day celebration in January has consisted of a small interracial group in our community marching together arm in arm to honor Dr. King's dream of becoming the Beloved Community. Together we embody a wonderful diversity of skin colors and social and economic backgrounds as we walk along, singing in unison, "We Shall Overcome Some Day." For a brief moment in these marches, I can see White people like me overcoming years of racial indoctrination, leaving aside old fears and prejudices about People of Color, and together celebrating our common humanity. White racial biases may die slowly in this country but die they must in order for us to become the land of the free and the home of the brave. As I continue with my own racial recovery process, I find myself appreciating the prayer written by Reinhold Niebuhr more than fifty years ago now:

"Nothing that is worth doing can be achieved in our lifetime; therefore, we must be saved by hope. Nothing which is true or beautiful or good makes complete sense in any immediate context of history; therefore, we must be saved by faith. Nothing

we do, however virtuous, can be accomplished alone; therefore, we must be saved by love. No virtuous act is quite as virtuous from the standpoint of our friend or foe as it is from our standpoint. Therefore, we must be saved by the final form of love which is forgiveness."

Amen!

APPENDIX
QUESTIONS TO STIMULATE DIALOGUE ON RACE AND WHITE RACIAL BIASES

1. What is your definition of "racism" and how have you experienced racism in your life?
2. Can you identify any racial biases that you harbor, either in the past or now?
3. What experiences in your life have shaped your racial identity or your perceptions about the racial identities of others?
4. Who or what has most profoundly shaped your perceptions about White people and People of Color?
5. When you think about White privileges that people of color do not enjoy, what comes to your mind?
6. How do you explain the disparities that exist today between White people and People of Color in terms of accumulated wealth, experiences with the criminal justice system, and encounters with law enforcement, educational achievement levels, and health issues?
7. What feelings do you have when you hear about our nation's history of racial genocide and violence, the enslavement of Africans, Jim Crow laws, racial segregation, and discrimination?
8. Why do you think many White people today are uncomfortable addressing issues of race?
9. How do you feel about the demographic changes occurring in

America that will likely leave White people in the minority in the next fifty years?

10. What do you think White people should be doing now to eradicate the vestiges of racism in America?

11. Who or what factors have been most significant in changing your attitudes about race or racial justice issues?

12. What issues or concerns would you have if one of your children or grandchildren were to marry someone with a different racial identity?

13. How many examples of racist public policies or institutional racism can you identify?

14. To what degree have you been exposed to the ideology of White superiority?

NOTES

Introduction

1   Joe R. Feagin, *The White Racial Frame: Centuries of Racial Framing and Counter-Framing*, Second Edition, Routledge, NY, 2013.
2   "What's Wrong With 'All Lives Matter'?" by George Yancy and Judith Butler, Interview of The Stone, January 12, 2015.

Chapter 1

1   "Facing Racism: A Vision of the Beloved Community," a document developed by the Initiative Team on Racism and Racial Violence of the Presbyterian Church (USA), 1997.

Chapter 2

1   Beverly Daniel Tatum, *Why Are All the Black Kids Sitting Together in the Cafeteria? And Other Conversations,* Revised and Updated,

New York: Basic Books, 2017.

2   Ibid. Joe R. Feagin, *The White Racial Frame: Centuries of Racial Framing and Counter-Framing.*

3   John McWhorter, "The Difference Between Racial Bias and White Supremacy," *Time*, November 29, 2016.

4   Ibid. McWhorter.

5   Imani Perry, *More Beautiful and More Terrible: The Embrace and Transcendence of Racial Inequality in the United States*, New York University Press.

6   Thomas Sowell, *Black Rednecks and White Liberals*, San Francisco: Encounter Books, 2005.

7   Charles M. Blow, "On Race: The Moral High Ground." *New York Times*, May 31, 2018.

Chapter 3

1   Robin DiAngelo, *White Fragility: Why It's So Hard For White People To Talk About Racism,* Beacon Press, 2018.

2   Nadira Hira, "Why the Fight Against Racism Has To Start With Owing It," *Newsweek*, August 22, 2019.

3   William K. Stephens, "Newcomers Alter Face of Exclusive Gross Pointe." *New York Times*, November 5, 1974.

4   "Declaration of Causes: February 2, 1861," Texas State Library and Archives Commission, https://www.tsl.texas.gov/ref/abouttx/secession/2feb1861.html.

5   Jefferson Davis, *The Rise and Fall of the Confederate Government*, Vol. 2 (1881) Reprinted New York: DaCapo Press, 1991, p. 161.

6   David Blight, *Race and Reunion: The Civil War in American Memory*, Harvard University Press, 2001.

7 Eric Foner, *The Story of American Freedom*, W. W. Norton & Co, 1998.
8 *American Institutions and Their Influence*, Alexis de Tocqueville, 1834.
9 David Brion Davis, *In the Image of God: Religious, Moral Values, and Our Heritage of Slavery*, Yale University Press, 2001.

Chapter 4

1 Ibram X. Kendi, *How to Be an Anti-Racist*, On World, 2019.
2 *The Nation*, Jamelle Bouie, "Reverse Discrimination: A Thorny Issue for Many Young People," April 26, 2012.
3 Ibid. Kendi.
4 https://www.loc.gov/resource/llst.022/?st=gallery.
5 "How Slavery Is Taught" in Teaching Hard History/American Slavery, www. SouthernPoverty Law Center.org.

Chapter 5

1 I have found Joe Feagin's explanation of the dynamics of what I generally call "White biases" and the grounding of White superiority in the idea of a Great Chain of Being to be especially helpful in understanding racist orientations that Whites have exhibited. So, I recommend the reading of *The White Racial Frame: Centuries of Racial Framing and Counter-Framing*, Routledge, Second Edition, 2013, in order to understand this perspective.

2   Ibid, Feagin, *The White Racial Frame: Centuries of Racial Framing and Counter-Framing*, Second Edition, Routledge, 2013, pp. 9–15.

3   David R. Roediger, *Working Toward Whiteness: How America's Immigrants Became White: The Strange Journey from Ellis Island to the Suburbs*, 2006, Basic.

4   Noam Gidron and Peter Hall, 2019 paper, "Populism as a Problem of Social Integration."

5   Ibram X. Kendi, *Stamped from the Beginning: The Definitive History of Racist Ideas*, 2016, Nation Books

6   "Mutual Relations of Masters and Slaves as Taught in the Bible": A Discourse Preached in First Presbyterian Church, Augusta, Georgia, January 6, 1861, by Rev. Joseph R. Wilson, Pastor, published by Steam Press of Chronicle and Sentinel, 1861.

7   "Declaration of Causes: February 2, 1861", Texas State Library and Archives Commission, https://www.tsl.texas.gov/ref/about-tx/secession/2feb1861.html.

8   Stokely Carmichael and Charles V. Hamilton, *Black Power: The Politics of Liberation in America*, 1967, Vintage Books.

9   Linda Faye Williams, *The Constraint of Race: Legacies of White Skin Privilege in America*, 2003, The Pennsylvania State University Press.

10 Peggy McIntosh, "White Privilege: Unpacking the Invisible Knapsack," *Peace and Freedom*, July/August 1989, pp. 10–12.

11 Andrea Smith, "Heteropatriarchy and the Three Pillars of White Supremacy: Rethinking Women of Color Organizing," July 2016, https://doi.org/10.1215/9780822373445-007.

12 W. E. B. DuBois, *The Soul of Black Folks*, 1903, AC McClurg & Co, Chicago.

13 http://www.coloursofresistance.org/498/white-supremacy-on-my-mind-learning-to-undermine-racism/.

14 Bell Hooks. AZQuotes.com, Wind and Fly LTD, 2017, http://www. azquotes.com/author/6871-Bell_Hooks, accessed January 09, 2017.

15 Cynthia Levine-Rasky, *Whiteness Fractured*, 2013, Routledge.

16 Derald Wing Sue, Overcoming Our Racism: The Journey to Liberation, 2003, John Wiley & Sons (this book has valuable exercises to undo racism).

17 Carol Anderson, *White Rage: The Unspoken Truth of Our Racial Divide,* 2016, Bloombury, New York.

Chapter 6

1 Malcolm X, *By Any Means Necessary*, Pathfinder, 1970.

2 Daniel Hill, *White Awake: An Honest Look at What It Means to Be White*, IVP Book, 2017.

3 Taken from a sermon given by John Metta on July 28, 2015, at Bethel Congregational United Church of Christ, Salmon City, Washington.

4 Ibid, Metta.

5 Linda Martin Alcoff, *Visible Identities: Race, Gender, and the Self*, 2006, Oxford University Press.

6 Linda M. Alcoff, "The Whiteness Question," http://www.alcoff. com/content/Whiteque.html.

7 "The Extent of Slave Ownership in the United States in 1860," Al Mackey, April 18, 2017, Student of the Civil War.

8 See the reprint of Mildred Lewis Rutherford's 1901 book *Truths of History: A Fair, Unbiased, Impartial, Unprejudices and Conscientious Study of History*, Forgotten Books, 2015 for the clear example of the White Southern mythology about how well slaves were treated on plantations.

9   "Did the Civil Rights Movement Go Wrong?" Jonathan Rauch, *New York Times*, January 17, 2020.

10 https://www.washingtonpost.com/opinions/2020/12/06/obamas-defund-police-comments-showcase-radical-cynicism/.

11 "White Racial Identity and Anti-Racist Education: A Catalyst for Change" by Sandra M. Lawrence and Beverly Daniel Tatum, https://www.teachingforchange.org/wp-content/uploads/2012/08/ec_whiteracialidentity_english.pdf.

Chapter 7

1   Ibid., http://www.coloursofresistance.org/498/white-supremacy-on-my-mind-learning-to-undermine-racism/.

Chapter 8

1   As a valuable resource for those wanting to become a White ally, I recommend *The White Ally Toolkit Workbook: Using Active Listening, Empathy, and Personal Storytelling to Promote Racial Equity*, First Edition by David W. Campt, PhD, I AM Publications, 2018.

BIBLIOGRAPHY

U.S. History

Cobb, James C. *Away Down South: A History of Southern Identity.* Oxford University Press, 2005.

Franklin, John Hope. *From Slavery to Freedom: A History of Negro Americans.* Alfred A. Knopf, 1974.

Isenberg, Nancy. *White Trash: The 400-Year Untold History of Class in America.* Viking, 2016.

Lepore, Jill. *These Truths: A History of the United States.* W. W. Norton & Company, 2018.

Mullane, Dierdre, ed. *Crossing the Dangerous Water: The Hundred Years of African American Writing.* Anchor Books, 1993.

Painter, Nell Irvin. *The History of White People.* W. W. Norton & Company, 2010.

Zinn, Howard. *People's History of the United States.* Harper Perennial, 2003.

Slavery

Berry, Dana Ramey. *The Price For Their Pound of Flesh: The Value of the Enslaved, from Womb to Grave, in the Building of a Nation.* Beacon Press, 2017.

Blumrosen, Alfred W., Blumrosen, Ruth G. and Blumrosen, Steven. *Slave Nation: How Slavery United the Colonies & Sparked the American Revolution.* Sourcebooks, 2005.

Spilsbury, Richard. *Slavery and the Slave Trade.* Heinemann Library, 2010.

Stampp, Kenneth M. *The Peculiar Institution: Slavery in the Ante-Bellum South.* Vintage Books, 1956.

Torget, Andrew J. *Seeds of Empire: Cotton, Slavery, and the Transformation of the Texas Borderlands 1800–1850.* University of North Carolina Press, 2015.

Civil War Interpretations

Blight, David W. *Race and Reunion: The Civil War in American Memory.* The Belnap Press of Harvard University Press, 2001

Brundage, W. Fitzhugh. *The Southern Past: A Clash of Race and Memory.* The Belnap Press of Harvard University Press, 2005.

Clinton, Catherine, ed. *Confederate Statues and Memorialization.* University of Georgia Press, 2019.

Dew, Charles B. *Apostles of Disunion: Southern Secession Commissioners and the Causes of the Civil War.* University of Virginia Press, 2001.

Foster, Gaines M. *Ghosts of the Confederacy: Defeat, the Lost Cause, and the Emergence of the New South*. Oxford University Press, 1987.

Gallagher, Gary W. and Nolan, Alan T., eds. *The Myth of the Lost Cause and Civil War History*. Indiana University Press, 2010.

Potter, David M. *The Impending Crisis: 1848–1861*. Harper Perennial, 1976.

Savage, Kirk. *Standing Soldiers, Kneeling Slaves: Race, War, and Monument in Nineteenth-Century America*. New Edition, Princeton University Press, 2018.

Wilson, Charles Reagan. *Baptized in Blood: The Religion of the Lost Cause 1865–1920*. University of Georgia Press, 2009.

Wooster, Ralph A. *The Secession Conventions of the South*. Princeton University Press, 1962.

Reconstruction Period

Blackmon, Douglas A. *Slavery By Another Name: The Re-Enslavement of Black Americans from the Civil War to World War II*. Anchor Books, 2009.

Carrigan, William D. *The Making of a Lynching Culture: Violence and Vigilantism in Central Texas, 1836-1916*. University of Illinois Press, 2004.

Foner, Eric. *Reconstruction: America's Unfinished Revolution, 1863–1877*. Harper Perennial, 2014.

Packard, Jerrold M. *American Nightmare: The History of Jim Crow*. St. Martin's Press, 2002.

Petre, Merline. *In Struggle Against Jim Crow: Lula B. White and the NAACP 1900–1957*. Texas A&M Press, 1999.

Rutherford, Mildred Lewis. *Truths of History: A Fair, Unbiased, Impartial, Unprejudiced and Conscientious Study of History*, 1901, reprinted by Forgotten Books, 2015.

Sutton, Robert K. and Latschar, John, eds. *The Reconstruction Era (1865–1877)*. Official National Park Handbook. Eastern National, 2016.

Woodward, C. Vann. *The Strange Career of Jim Crow*. Oxford University Press, 2002.

Civil Rights Era

Bates, Daisy. *The Long Shadow of Little Rock: A Memoir*. The University of Arkansas Press, 1986.

Carmichael, Stokely and Hamilton, Charles V. *Black Power: The Politics of Liberation in America*. Vintage Books, 1967.

Chafe, William H., Gavins, Raymond, and Korstad, Robert, eds. *Remembering Jim Crow: African Americans Tell about Life in the Segregated South*. Includes documentary CD recordings. The New Press, 2001.

Clarke, Terrence. *The Arena of Truth: Conflict in Black and White*. A/T Publishers, 2019.

Cone, James. *Martin & Malcolm & America: A Dream or a Nightmare*. Orbis Books, 2nd printing, 2020

David, Townsend. *Weary Feet, Rested Souls: A Guided History of the Civil Rights Movement*. WW Norton & Company, 1998.

Hurst, Rodney L., Sr. *It Was Never About a Hot Dog and a Coke!: A Personal Account of the 1960 Sit-in Demonstrations in Jacksonville, Florida and Ax Handle Saturday*. Wingspan Press, 2008.

King, Martin Luther, Jr. *Where Do We Go from Here: Chaos or Community?* Beacon Press, 1968.

LaNier, Carlotta Walls. *A Mighty Long Way: My Journey to Justice at Little Rock Central High School.* One World Books, 2009.

Michel, Gregg L. *Struggling for a Better South: The Southern Student Organizing Committee 1964–1969.* Palgrave MacMillan, 2004.

Rabby, Glenda Alice. *The Pain and the Promise: The Struggle for Civil Rights in Tallahassee, Florida.* University of Georgia Press, 1999.

Washington, James M., ed. *A Testament Of Hope: The Essential Writings and Speeches of Martin Luther King, Jr.* Harper, 1986.

X, Malcolm. *By Any Means Necessary.* Pathfinder, 1992.

Racism in America

Anderson, Margaret and Collins, Patricia Hill. *Race, Class and Gender: An Anthology.* Wadsworth, 2001.

Bonilla-Silva, Eduardo. *Racism Without Racists: Color-Blind Racism and the Persistence of Racial Inequality in America.* Fifth Edition. Rowman and Littlefield, 2018.

Coates, Ta-Nehisi. *Between the World and Me.* Spiegel & Grau, 2015.

Cone, James. *The Cross and the Lynching Tree.* Orbis Books, 2017.

Cone, James H. *God of the Oppressed.* Revised Edition, Orbis Books, 1997.

Conrad, Earl. *The Invention of the Negro.* Paul S. Eriksson, 1966.

D'Souza, Dinesh. *The End of Racism: Principles for a Multiracial Society.* The Free Press, 1995.

Davis, David Brion. *In the Image of God: Religion, Moral Values, and Our Heritage of Slavery.* Yale University Press, 2001.

DuBois, W. E. B. *Dusk of Dawn: An Essay toward an Autobiography of a Race Concept*. Fourteenth Printing, Transaction Publishers, 2009.

DuBois, W. E. B. *The Souls of Black Folk*. Dover Publications, 1903.

Feagin, Joe R. *Racist America: Roots, Current Realities, and Future Reparations*. Third Edition. Routledge, 2014.

Feagin, Joe R. *Systematic Racism: A Theory of Oppression*. Routledge, 2006.

Frederickson, George M. *Racism: A Short History*. Princeton University Press, 2002.

Gates, Henry Louis, Jr. and West, Cornel. *The Future of Race*. Vintage Books, 1996.

Grier, William H. and Cobbs, Price M. *Back Rage*. Basic Books, 1968.

Hacker, Andrew. *Two Nations: Black and White, Separate, Hostile, Unequal*. Charles Scribner's Sons, 1992.

Kendi, Ibram X. *Stamped From the Beginning: The Definitive History of Racist Ideas in America*. Nation Books, 2016.

McGhee, Heather. *The Sum of Us: What Racism Cost Everyone and How We Can Prosper Together*. One World, 2021.

Myrdal, Gunnar. *An American Dilemma: The Negro Problem and Modern Democracy, Vols I & II*. Harper and Row, Transaction Publishers, 1944.

Perry, Imani. *More Beautiful and More Terrible: The Embrace and Transcendence of Racial Inequality in the United States*. New York University Press, 2011.

Richardson, Heather Cox. *How the South Won the Civil War: Oligarchy, Democracy, and the Continuing Fight For the Soul of America*. Oxford University Press, New York, 2020.

Roberts, Dorothy. *Fatal Invention: How Science, Politics, and Big Business Re-Create Race in the Twenty-First Century*. The New Press, 2011.

Stoddard, Lothrop. *The Rising Tide of Color Against White World-Supremacy*. Charles Scribner's Sons, 1922.

Singh, Anneliese. *The Racial Healing Handbook: Practical Activities to Help You Challenge Privilege, Confront Systemic Racism, and Engage in Collective Healing*, New Harbinger Publishers, 2019.

Sue, Derald Wing. *Overcoming Our Racism: The Journey to Liberation.* Jossey Bass, 2003.

Sue, Derald Wing. *Race Talk and the Conspiracy of Silence: Understanding and Facilitating Difficult Dialogues on Race*. Wiley Press, 2015.

Wallis, Jim. *America's Original Sin: Racism, White Privilege, and the Bridge to a New America*. Brazos Press, 2016.

Wilkerson, Isabell. *Caste: The Origins of Our Discontents*. Random House, 2020.

Yancy, George. *Backlash: What Happens When We Talk Honestly About Race in America*. Rowman and Littlefield, 2018.

White Identity

Anderson, Carol. *White Rage: The Unspoken Truth of Our Racial Divide*. Bloomsbury, 2016.

Battalora, Jacqueline. *Birth of a White Nation: The Invention of White People and Its Relevance Today*. Strategic Book Publishing and Rights Co., 2013.

Billings, David. *Deep Denial: The Persistence of White Supremacy in United States History and Life*.

Crandall, Dostic & Douglass Books, Inc., 2016.

Connelly, Kerry. *Good White Racist?: Confronting Your Role in Racial Injustice*. Westminster John Knox Press, 2020.

DiAngelo, Robin. *White Fragility: Why It's So Hard For White People To Talk About Racism*. Beacon Press, 2018.

Dyson, Michael Eric. *Tears We Cannot Stop: A Sermon to White America*. St Martin's Press, 2017.

Feagin, Joe R. *The White Racial Frame: Centuries of Racial Framing and Counter-Framing*. Second Edition, Routledge, 2013.

Fletcher, Jeannine Hill. *The Sin of White Supremacy: Christianity, Racism, and Religious Diversity in America*. Orbis Books, 2017.

Fleming, Crystal M. *How To Be Less Stupid About Race: On Racism, White Supremacy and the Racial Divide*. Beacon Press, 2018.

Hill, Daniel. *White Awake: An Honest Look at What It Means to Be White*, IVP Book, 2017.

Helsel, Carolyn B. *Anxious to Talk about It: Helping White Christians Talk Faithfully about Racism*. Chalice Press, 2017.

Irving, Debby. *Waking Up White: and Finding Myself in the Story of Race*. Elephant Room Press, 2014.

Jensen, Robert. *The Heart of Whiteness: Confronting Race, Racism, and White Privilege*. City Lights Publishers, 2005.

Jones, Robert P. *White Too Long: The Legacy of White Supremacy in American Christianity*. Simon & Schuster, 2020.

Kendall, Frances E. *Understanding White Privilege: Creating Pathways To Authentic Relationships Across Race, Second Edition*. Routledge, 2013.

Lipsitz, George. *The Possessive Investment in Whiteness: How White People Profit from Identity Politics*. Twentieth Anniversary Edition. Temple University Press, Philadelphia, 2018.

Middleton, Roediger, Shaffer, eds. *The Construction of Whiteness: An Interdisciplinary Analysis of Race Formation and the Meaning of White Identity*. University Press of Mississippi, 2016.

Oluo, Ijeoma. *Mediocre: The Dangerous Legacy of White Male America*. Seal Press, 2020.

Oluo, Ijeoma. *So You Want To Talk About Race*. Seal Press, 2019.

Roediger, David R., ed. *Black on White: Black Writers on What It Means to Be White*. Schocken Books, 1998.

Rothenberg, Paula S. *White Privilege: Essential Reading on the Other Side of Racism*. Third Edition. Worth Publishers, 2008.

Singley, Bernestine, ed. *When Race Becomes Real: Black and White Writers Confront Their Personal Histories*. Lawrence Hill Books, 2002.

Tatum, Beverly Daniel. *Why Are All the Black Kids Sitting Together in the Cafeteria? And Other Conversations About Race*. Basic Books, 2017.

Williams, Linda Faye. *The Constraint of Race: Legacies of White Skin Privilege in America*. Penn State Press, 2003.

Wise, Tim. *Dear White America: Letter to A New Minority*. City Lights Books, 2012.

Dismantling White Racial Biases

Brandt, Joseph. *Understanding and Dismantling Racism: The Twenty-First Century Challenge to White America*. Fortress Press, 2007.

Campt, David W. *The White Ally Toolkit Workbook: Using Active Listening, Empathy, and Personal Storytelling to Promote Racial Equity*. I Am Publications, 2018.

Eberhardt, Jennifer L. *Biased: Uncovering the Hidden Prejudice That Shapes What We See, Think, and Do*. Viking, 2019.

Katz, Judith H. *White Awareness: Handbook for Anti-Racism Training*. Second Edition. University of Oklahoma Press, 2003.

Kendi, Ibram X. *How To Be An Anti-Racist*. One World, 2019.

Kivel, Paul. *Uprooting Racism: How White People Can Work for Racial Justice, 3rd Edition*. New Society Publishers, 2011.

Morrison, Latasha. *Be the Bridge: Pursuing God's Heart for Racial Reconciliation*. Waterbrook, 2019.

Parker, Robin and Chambers, Pamela Smith. *The Anti-Racism Cookbook: A Recipe Guide for Conversations About Race That Goes Beyond Covered Dishes and "Kum-Bah-Ya."* Crandall, Dostie, and Douglas Books, 2005.

Saad, Layla R. *Me and White Supremacy: Combat Racism, Change the World, and Become a Good Ancestor*. Sourcebooks, 2020.

Singleton, Glenn E. *More Courageous Conversations about Race*. Corwin, 2013.

Tisby, Jemar. *How To Fight Racism: Courageous Christianity and the Journey Toward Racial Justice*. Zondervan, 2021.

Tochluk, Shelly. *Witnessing Whiteness: First Steps Toward An Antiracist Practice and Culture*. Rowman and Littlefield Education, 2008.

Other

Fanon, Frantz. Translated by Philcox, Richard. *Black Skin, White Masks*. Grove Press, 2008.

Gergel, Richard. *Unexamined Courage: The Blinding of Sgt. Isaac Woodard and the Awakening of President Truman and Judge J. Waites Waring*. Sarah Crichton Books, 2019.

Hicks, Brian. *In Darkest South Carolina: J. Waties Waring and the Secret Plan that Sparked a civil rights Movement*. Evening Post Books, 2018.

Horwitz, Tony. *Confederates in the Attic: Dispatches from the Unfinished Civil War*. Vintage, 1999.

King, Larry L. *Confessions of a White Racist*. The Viking Press, 1971.

Morrison, Toni, ed. *James Baldwin: Collected Essays*. The Library of America, 1998.

Articles

newrepublic.com/article/122843/
constitutionally-slavery-indeed-national-institution
Article of same name by Lawrence Goldstone, September 17, 2015
www.splcenter.org/fighting-hate/intelligence-report/2000/
neo-confederates
Article entitled "The Neo-confederates" from the Intelligence Report of the Southern Poverty Law Center, September 15, 2000
www.washingtonpost.com/outlook/five-myths-about-why-the-south-seceded/2011/01/03/ABHr6jD_story.html
Article of same name by James W. Loewen, February 26, 2011
www.washingtonpost.com/posteverything/wp/2015/07/01/why-do-people-believe-myths-about-the-confederacy-because-our-textbooks-and-monuments-are-wrong/
Article of the same name by James W. Loewen, July 1, 2015
http://www.newsobserver.com/opinion/op-ed/article31123988.html
Article entitled "Commemorating North Carolina's Anti-Confederate Heritage, Too" by Timothy B. Tyson, August 16. 2015
/alcalde.texasexes.org/2015/08/seeing-race/
Article of same name by Leonard Moore, in *Alcalde,* September/October 2015
www.washingtonpost.com/lifestyle/style/the-souths-confederate-monument-problem-is-not-going-away/2016/05/08/b0258e4a-05af-11e6-a12f-ea5aed7958dc_story.html

Article of the same name by Monica Hesse, May 8, 2016
http://www.theatlantic.com/politics/archive/2016/04/the-stub-
   born-persistence-of-confederate-monuments/479751/

www.ingramcontent.com/pod-product-compliance
Lightning Source LLC
Chambersburg PA
CBHW070102030426
42335CB00016B/1981